WHO ARE YOU?

How understanding who you are will change the world.

OLIVER COX

WHO ARE YOU?

FROM PLATO TO CARL JUNG, THROUGH EVERY ORGANISED RELIGION ON EARTH THE IDEA OF THE TRUE SELF HAS BEEN ASSERTED.

DO YOU KNOW WHO YOU ARE?

THIS BOOK WILL GUIDE YOU BACK TO YOUR TRUE SELF AND EXPLAIN WHY UNDERSTANDING WHO YOU REALLY ARE, WILL CHANGE THE WORLD.

Disclaimer: The author and publisher of this book and eBook have used their best efforts in preparing this book and eBook. The author and publisher make representation or warranties with respect to the accuracy, applicability, fitness, or completeness of the contents of this book and eBook. The information contained in this book and eBook is strictly for educational purposes only. Therefore, if you wish to apply ideas contained in this eBook, you are taking full responsibility for your actions.

Oliver J Cox Publishing 2022

Cover design by Sahidul88737, @99designs.

A HUGE THANK YOU TO MY AMAZING FAMILY, LYNDON MALLET, JIM JEALOUS, AND ALL MY PATIENTS. THIS BOOK WOULD NOT HAVE HAPPENED WITHOUT YOU. MUCH LOVE.

Contents

FOR ALL WHO SEEK TO RE-
IMAGINE THE WORLD,

IN FREEDOM AND HUMILITY,
AS ONE.

WE ARE NOT TRYING TO BE ENLIGHTENED;

WE ARE ONLY TRYING TO BE OURSELVES.

There are guided mediations specifically connected to this book and my meditation courses available for free on my YouTube Channel: The Family Osteopath.

If you would like to contact me directly my email address is: Oliver@Familyosteopath.co.uk, or you can contact me via my Facebook page: Centering Around the Edges. Thank you. Oliver.

I am writing this book as a promise to the Ocean and because keeping quiet when you think things are wrong is a polite form of lying.

Chapter One

Our 'Trip' Begins.

There is a lecture that I like to listen to when the mood takes me given by a man named Jiddu Krishnamurti. It was delivered in 1978 in Madras, now known as Chennai, on the southeast coast of India. The talk gets underway with no pleasantries; straight to it, as is his custom. He begins:

> *"We are concerned with the transformation psychologically inwardly of human beings. We human beings have created this monstrous world. Almost insane. Destructive, violent. Unless our Consciousness undergoes a radical transformation psychologically really, there is no hope for man. Obviously..."*

As abrupt a statement as this is, to my mind it is true. This book is a journey to discover where we are as a race now. To find out whether it's possible for us to change inwardly, as suggested, in a way that would change our fate and that of the Natural World of which we are a part. I invite you to come on a journey with me to discover for yourself whether we can change fundamentally, psychologically, internally?

We start with the not so small question of What is thinking? So, buckle up; we are going in.

Our journey together begins with the interesting, strange, and turbulent life of a man called Timothy Francis Leary. If I was aware of Timothy Leary in my younger life it was as a figure on a flyer for a nightclub, or on a documentary about the 'summer of love'. The figure had no real substance in my awareness of him. He was a man with flowers around his neck stood in a park in San Francisco encouraging us to *"Turn on, tune in, drop out"*.

I started to become personally more interested in his ideas through the books of John Higgs. John wrote a biography on Leary early on in his writing career – *"I have America Surrounded"* - and has subsequently had Leary's models of consciousness within his writing - alongside Robert Anton Wilson - in many of his subsequent books.

Leary himself wrote an autobiography suitable enough called *"Flashbacks"*! Alongside the books, the web is awash with forums and opinions about him. We are left with a satisfying enigma of myth, legend and solid academic output.

John Higg's book begins with Leary's daring and successful escape from jail in America where he is spirited away by a political group and out of the country. As amazing as this story is, it is just one of many.

This is not our beginning point though. We are seeking to examine what Leary has to say about the nature of thinking or consciousness, and how he arrived at these models of thought.

Timothy Leary is Born on October 22, 1920, he was the only child of Abigail Ferris and Timothy Leary (Tote to his friends).

Abigail came from a strictly puritanical Catholic farming home in Massachusetts, America. Tim's description of his Aunt Dudu and his Grandfather gives you an idea of how he viewed this side of the family. *"I never knew my grandparents on the Ferris side. They died in the influenza outbreak of 1918, leaving the diminished acreage and two farmhouses to my Aunt Dudu, a timid, fanatically religious gnome who futilely tried to direct family affairs with Irish-village piety, sitting on a couch all day clicking her false teeth, mumbling prayers, and reading Catholic tracts. As befitted her venerable status as ruler of the household, Aunt Dudu slept in the master bedroom, called "Grandfather's Room" in honor of the doughty little farmer-tyrant who built it."*

His Dad, Tote, came from an affluent - and as Tim say's a *"hot and sassy"* family - based in the city of Springfield, Massachusetts. His grandfather (Also called Tim) was a professor, a medic, and an owner of real estate. He was thought of as the richest Irish American in Western Massachusetts to those that knew of him. The only direct piece of advice given to Tim by Grandfather Leary was perhaps poignant *"Never do anything like anyone else, boy."*

Tim's childhood was, by all accounts, a bit lonely in that he had few friends of his own age to play with. He was brought up in the Catholic tradition, as was typical of most Irish families of the time. Like many of us, he was a dreamer and often escaped his life through his imagination playing out fantastical role play adventures. A past time that maybe he never stopped!

When Tim turned 14, his grandfather passed away. Everyone on the Leary side had awaited this time with great anticipation. Envisioning a future of great wealth and luxury. It was not to be. The family discovered that all his wealth had been lost. At this unfortunate revelation, Tim's Dad went out to get drunk and did not enter his life again for 23 years.

After an unsuccessful, turbulent, and interesting career in the Army, Tim enrolled to study psychiatry at Berkeley, California, in 1946. His early career was very successful. At this time, he was responsible for several theories still considered and used today, such as:

'Interpersonal diagnosis' which is a method of categorising patients based on personality type. This was a precursor to the Myres-Briggs assessment used now for hiring, or declining people jobs, if the latter is appropriate.

Another of his theories asserted that the idea put forward by psychology at the time, of normal, was just a representation of the white, middle-class values shared by most white, middle-class psychologists that made up the industry in America. It encouraged the profession to stop focussing on symptoms and start to look at the patient's environment and circumstances instead. What was going on in their lives?

He asserted that what was considered to be abnormal, neurotic or psychotic behaviour was just a way for the individual to survive in the world. We will find out that the compensations we make in order to survive are of significant importance, and have a substantial effect on how we think, act, view the world and ourselves and, importantly, how healthy we are. It was an important theory.

He also said that the patient should not be considered a victim and should not be encouraged to look for a source of their problems. Instead, they should accept responsibility for their lives and their own reactions to events.

The problems began when Tim started to look at how effective psychology was at the time. He and his team had been carrying out studies on how effective their treatments were, and the results were not good. No matter what kind of psychotherapy they used, a third of patients would get better, a third would stay the same, and a third would deteriorate further. Control groups, where no care was given, showed precisely the same results! What they were doing was not working.

At this time, Tim was married to a lady called Marianne Busch and lived in a house in Berkeley Hills overlooking San Francisco across the water. The couple had two children, Susan and Jack. For Tim, life took the form of lots of work and socialising. Alcohol was a dominant theme in their lives, with a constant stream of parties and get-togethers. In this environment, Tim started having an affair with a colleague. It was said that Marianne knew of this, but she never challenged him about it directly.

Then in 1955, when Susan would have been 9 and jack 7, they woke to find that Marianne had taken her own life by sitting in the garage with the car engine running. Her note read: *"My Darling, I cannot live without your love. I have loved life but have lived through you. The children will grow up wondering about their Mother. I love them so much, and please tell them that. Please be good to them. They are so dear."*

We can only attempt to imagine what the fall-out from this horrifically sad event felt like. Still, we understand it sent shock waves through the whole family, not least the children. The course of their lives was changed forever. What happened immediately afterwards, in short, included a quick marriage and separation from the lady Tim was having an affair with, a sabbatical from work, and a move to Spain.

This period according to the children, and Tim, was unsurprisingly not a positive one. It culminated in Tim becoming very ill due, amongst other things, to the damp conditions where they were living. A serious illness that initially led to Tim's head and face swelling up, with the added formation of water blisters.

Later, his son Jack reported, *"Tim's head was twice the size, completely swollen up, incredible! He couldn't see; his eyes were completely shut!"* Jack and Susan were sent to some American friends living up the coast. At the same time, Tim checked into a warmer and drier hotel room to convalesce.

Doctors did not know what was happening and had no working diagnosis, never having seen anything like it previously. As time went on, Tim's condition worsened with swelling and blisters covering his whole body. He started to smell of decay. It was likely that Tim was suffering from Pemphigus, acute necrotizing ulcerative gingivitis. A very serious illness now, and definitely then.

That evening Tim just 'let go'. He later wrote, *"I died. I let go. I surrendered. I slowly let every tie to my old life slip away. My career, my ambitions, my home. My identity. The guilts. The wants. With a sudden snap, all the ropes of my social life were gone."*

Then came an incredible feeling of freedom. Tim felt, at that time, that a spiritual event had taken place. This kind of experience at very extreme moments in someone's life is something shared by many people. It is the death of the false self, created through thinking, brought on by extreme pressure.

The following day the swelling was easing. Tim was recovering from the illness. He felt he had been given a new lease of life, and he was filled with renewed optimism and confidence. His previous work at Berkley and his previous research and books were enough to secure a new job at Harvard University's centre for Personality research. Professor McClelland - Tim's employer at Harvard – liked the fact Tim was *"urging that we emphasize inner potential and personal growth through self-reliance, so patients avoid dependence on authoritarian doctors and dogmas."* Tim, Jack, and Susan returned to America. It was 1959.

Tim settled well back in Massachusetts. He was home and close to his Mum again. Tim quickly became a well-liked and respected professor to his students. Two colleagues at Harvard, Richard Alpert (later known as Ram Dass) and Frank Barron (an old friend), and Tim agreed they would holiday together in the summer. They set off for Mexico in the summer break with Richard Alpert flying the Leary's in his light aircraft.

While in Mexico, Tim was talked into trying magic mushrooms 'psilocybin'. Frank Barron had previously mentioned there use and believed they might help in creating behaviour change in patients. One of that day's attendees, Bruce, was assigned the job of the sober observer. *"After half an hour, the effects of the drug started, and the world just came alive. Tim looked at Bruce, who was diligently writing down his observations and was struck by the realisation that Bruce had no idea at all what he was observing. He found this realisation incredibly funny, and the earnestness and detachment of the scientific community suddenly appeared to him as ludicrous ignorance. How could they even begin to understand something that they were so separated from?"*

From the above experience and numerous others, using every kind of psychedelic drug, Tim starts to form firm ideas around the question: What is thinking or Consciousness?

To describe this idea, he coins the term *"Reality Tunnel"* which he expresses as follows:

As soon as our senses are able, we start to take in the world around us and interpret it. We take in our family, our culture, education, current theories and concepts, television, books, and everything in between. From this mosaic of experiences, we build an image of ourselves and the world around us in the mind. This has to be seen as unique to the individual brain. It is a fragmented and undoubtedly incomplete picture of the universe, a hotch-potch of what we happen to have come across directly or indirectly.

It is within this Reality Tunnel that we navigate ourselves through life. Therefore, the world, seen in this tunnel is not reality but a mere model created in our own brains. This is the only reality for a vast number of people in the world; maybe you too?

My Cat is offering up an excellent living example of this as I write. Last week we added an 11-month-old collie to our family who is very sweet and gentle and has no specific interest in my Cat. My Cat's mind, though, believes that we have bought a wolf who is waiting to tear her apart at the first opportunity. This is a reality that is real to her at this time. And no, I don't think she needs LSD!

Chapter Two

The Unusual Life of Krishnamurti

We will leave Tim for a while and turn our attention to someone who has similar, but for me vitally different ideas, about Consciousness.

Jiddu Krishnamurti was born the eighth child of Jiddu and Sanjeevamma Narayaniah on May 11 1895. They were a high-caste Shaivite Brahmin family based in Madanapalle, Andhra Pradesh, South India.

Traditionally in India, the eighth born son is named Krishna, as Lord Krishna is believed to have been.

Early perceptions of the young Krishna were not all positive. He was considered aloof to the point of not being present.

Like Tim, Krishna was a dreamer. Later Krishna would tell stories of being regularly beaten at school for not concentrating and being unable to answer questions. He would then be told to stand for hours on the school porch until his brother Nitya would eventually collect him at the end of the day.

His Mother always believed that Krishna was in some way special and destined to be important. She was, by all accounts, a warm and loving mum who was very fond of her son. Krishna's Dad is described as a more detached figure. The family certainly had its fair share of hardship, with only 6 of their 11 children surviving into adulthood.

Things would get decidedly worse for the young Krishna and his siblings when his Mother dies. Krishna was only 10 at that time and would later describe his Mother as *"to a certain extent*

Psychic". He related how she would frequently see and speak to his sister, who had died at the age of 20.

Krishna himself reported seeing his Mother after she died and hearing the sound of her bangles following him to school.

Krishna's father was a Hindu and a Theosophist; spirituality and the occult were commonplace within the Krishnamurti family.

Theosophy was to play a crucial part in the family's history. The movement began in New York in 1875, started by Helena Blavatsky, a Russian emigrant, and Colonel Henry Olcott. It brought together their interpretation of Hinduism, Buddhism, and occult ideas that were unique to Blavatsky. Its main aim was to bring together East and West to form a new universal brotherhood of man. There was no specific dogma other than wanting to be part of the said brotherhood. Anyone could join.

To say that Helena Blavatsky was a character would be putting it lightly. She claimed that since childhood, she had been visited by a tall, dark protector who she identified as Master Morya, as well as by other spiritual beings. She called these figures the Masters and believed they had been born and died like anyone else but now had the purpose of helping mankind in challenging times.

Blavatsky claimed to be an earthly messenger for them.

Whatever we may choose to believe, Blavatsky certainly understood the idea of myth and of theatre. Many great stories followed her around. For example, a captain of a ship on which she was a passenger recounted that he had *"seen her light her cigar, without matches or other observable assistance, while standing at the rail in the midst of a furious storm. Every other living creature had been driven below deck."*

Another story involved Blavatsky helping Garibaldi in his efforts to unify Italy.

Col. Henry Olcott reported seeing her left arm where it had been broken in two places by a sabre. Accompanying these wounds were two musket bullet wounds and a stab wound near the heart caused by a stiletto. Hers was no ordinary life.

Other important figures in the movement, whose fates became intertwined with Krishna, were Charles Leadbeater (Who also laid claim to extraordinary life events and the ability to communicate with the Masters) and Annie Besant, a well-liked, respected person who successfully grew Theosophy Internationally.

Theosophy was a significant movement in its time with tens of thousands of members around the world. The movement had changed Headquarters from New York to Adyar in Southern India soon after its beginning.

Krishna's father had secured work at the Adyar Headquarters after retiring from a government tax role in 1907. The family, now consisting of four brothers and their father, lived in a shabby cottage outside the gates.

A large part of Blavatsky's and Leadbeater's ideology was that there would be the coming of a new 'World Teacher'. To put this into perspective, they claimed that Lord Maitreya, a figure taken from Buddhist mythology, would come to Earth as a messianic figure. It was contended that Maitreya had previously incarnated onto the Earth as Lord Krishna and Jesus. Not so much a big claim as a colossal one. It was told that the Master's would highlight a person who would become, with training, the vehicle for this divine event. It was Jiddu Krishnamurti who was bestowed this dubious honour.

Both he and his brother Nitya (who was deemed a vital part of Krishna's development by the Masters) were removed from their family altogether. They were never to return.

There was again surprise from some of the staff present at Adyar that Krishna was this supposed figure, as outwardly he appeared: *"scrawny, dirty, cough racked, lice-ridden, crooked toothed with rickety legs". His tutors reported that he was "dim-witted".*

When we think about this, it is hard not to notice the proximity of Krishna to the Theosophical headquarters. This was convenient, with the corresponding advantage that they had a level of control over his father as an employee.

Whatever the facts were, Krishna himself would always maintain that he was not conditioned by Theosophical ideas or any other education. (I know personally that being a dreamer at school, and in my case also dyslexic, means you can ignore a lot of lessons, but maybe not all of them!) I still believe that my dyslexia did limit the conditioning that was applied to me, and I am very grateful for this.

In 1911 the brothers were taken to England with Annie Besant to further their education. They would not return to India for ten years. At this time, the Theosophical movement had announced that they had found the 'World Teacher', so their arrival in England was accompanied by much excitement and fanfare.

Although Krishna and Nitya had spent some time adjusting to their new life in Adyar. It must have been challenging to be suddenly thrust into British life, even more so the British upper classes. There are pictures taken at this time with the two brothers sitting in fitted suits and ties with perfectly styled hair. This is a clue as to how different life had become for the two boys, who had lived previously in surroundings unimaginable to the British elite with whom they were now associated.

1912 bought legal action from the brothers' father to have then returned to his custody. This was fought and lost by the Theosophy movement in the courts of India but eventually won by Annie Besant on appeal in London.

While this was happening, the brothers were living a life of luxury, Krishna having been given an extremely generous weekly allowance of £500 for life from a Mrs Dodge, a wealthy and enthusiastic member of the Theosophist movement. She would also give him the house and land that Krishna would live in most of his life, which was in Ojai, California.

More gifts arrived from other supporters of the movement, including an 18th-century castle in Holland with 5,000 acres of pine forest! There was a time when all this materialism and wealth seemed to affect Krishna, and there were worries within the Theosophical movement. I am not sure whether, in the same situation, any of us would not have wobbled a bit!

It is hard to know when Krishna started to move away from the ideology and ideas within Theosophy. Still, we know it happened prior to Nitya's death. Nitya, we know, never did doubt the teachings or the importance that these ideas placed on his brother. Nitya had started to become ill in 1921 after a nasty bout of chickenpox just before returning for the first time to India, where he would go on to contract tuberculosis in both lungs.

In India, the reality of being presented as a divine figure was brought firmly home to Krishna. Large numbers of adoring people would greet him, reaching out to touch his clothes and feet. He would have known that the messianic premonition had not come to being. Not long after, while in Australia, a few people were pointing him out and laughing at the idea of him being a messiah. Krishna later said he wanted to laugh too at the ridiculousness of the situation, but was not able to at that time.

Internally Krishna was very conflicted, based on not wanting to abuse the trust of his carers, his brother, and close friends. It was hard for him to know how to continue. Due to Nitya's worsening health, the brothers were to find themselves heading for the first time to America. The warm, dry air of California was deemed the perfect place for Nitya to convalesce.

The brother's first view of America was San Francisco in 1922. A professor, ironically from the University of Berkeley, met them off the boat. This is where Timothy Leary would study and work 24 years later.

While on campus, Krishna was immediately struck by the open nature of the American students; there was a great sense of freedom and equality. Gone was the oppressive class system of England and the Caste system of India. It was also the first time in years the brothers were free from their custodians.

They travelled down to Ojai, inland in the hills from Santa Barbara. They stayed in a cottage on the grounds of the house that would become Krishna's home for years to come.

Here they were looked after by a young American girl called Rosalind Williams, who had previously worked on the estate. She was only 19 but proved to be very capable of caring for both of the brothers. Nitya and Rosalind would, in time, fall in love and Rosalind would remain in Krishna's life for many years to come.

As Rosalind now took over the care of Nitya, Krishna was free to roam and rest in the glorious, quiet, and natural surroundings.

Here, Krishna begins to concentrate spiritually, having the time to think and meditate freely without interruption. During this time, Krishna was to have what is called a 'samadhi' experience lasting three days. On the third day, Nitya reported feeling a great force filling the house. Even though Rosalind kept everything very clean, Krishna complained of filth in the house and in his bed. He allowed no one near him during this experience and huddled in the corner of the bedroom.

Eventually, later that evening, Nitya, Rosalind and another friend convinced Krishna to sit outside to cool down from the hot day.

Krishna sat below a tree and began to chant mantrams. Nitya was reminded of a moment long before when the two brothers had seen a painted representation of the Buddha, and both of them had felt they had received a divine thought. At that moment, Nitya felt the same presence and saw a great star above the tree. Nitya related that Rosalind repeatedly said the words *"Do you see him?"* whom Nitya took to mean the Divine Bodhisattva. After the event, which lasted about 30 minutes, Krishna rose and walked towards them, whereupon Rosalind fainted. Later she would not remember seeing anything, but they all reported hearing music.

Through later reports from Rosalind, we know that in 1925 Krishna and Nitya had stopped speaking due to Krishna's changing attitude towards Theosophy and their ideology. It was Nitya's death in October of that year that would be the final fracture. Krishna and Rosalind were on their way to India after being assured by Charles Leadbeater that the Masters had confirmed Nitya would live. While on the boat, Rosalind would be visited in her sleep by Nitya, wearing a white scarf around his neck. She reports that he was *"in good spirits"* and *"told her many things"*. To be sure that Rosalind didn't discount the experience, he told her to remember the scarf.

The next morning news of Nitya's death the previous night reached them on the boat. Subsequent questioning of the lady who was caring for Nitya confirmed that it was her scarf and that she had given it to Nitya to ease his sore neck. This was the last time Krishna would be swayed by stories of the Masters – and here we arrive at the awakening of a real teacher. Described later by the Dalai Lama as *"One of the greatest thinkers of the age"*, he put forward a message of complete freedom from thought and from conditioning. He now refuted publicly the claims that he was a World Teacher and instead urged that each person find their own path and find their own true self.

Chapter Three

One statue, two angles

Both Krishna and Tim were living in California at the same time. They shared a close friend and ally in the British Author Aldous Huxley, who was a vital confidant to both men.

Krishna and Tim were in complete agreement that the average person's reality was an illusion created by the mind and that they were not, on the whole, aware of it.

They agreed that it was the inability to understand and to see past this false reality, created by the brain, that was the source of the World's conflicts and problems. If the world was going to change, it had to come from a complete internal, psychological change happening within individuals.

These views were not new. We can find similar ideas from the Greek philosopher Plato in the 5th century B.C. when he says that the World we are aware of is like *"shadows on the wall of the cave"*. In the Tao Te Ching, credited to Lao Tzu in the 6th Century BC, one of the great spiritual texts reads, *"Can you coax your mind from its wandering and keep to the original oneness"*. In Hinduism and Buddhism, this illusion of the mind is known as *"Maya"*.

Tim and Krishna were very different people who had very different ideas on how to bring this realisation to the masses. They also disagreed on whether there was 'Intelligence' outside of the brain.

Tim, as we know, felt that the way to achieve this end was the mass use of drugs, particularly psychedelics such as LSD. He argued that LSD could enable the individual to reject one reality tunnel and imprint another, when needed or wanted. A person could step from one reality to another.

The trouble with this viewpoint is not whether or not it was possible, but that it was all taking place in the landscape of thinking. Therefore, because it was still centred around the ego, with all its selfish wants and desires, it was inherently unstable. If you were coming from a place of mental instability in the first place, it was anyone's guess where you would end up.

In 1904 Aleister Crowley, to whom Leary felt a deep connection, published a book called 'The book of the law'.

The story goes that While in Egypt, Crowley's wife Edith went into a trance state and repeatedly said, *"They're waiting for you!"*. When Crowley asked who was waiting, Edith said the name Horus. Edith had no personal knowledge of this figure but was able to answer multiple questions in regard to him.

As a final test Crowley took Edith to the Bulaq Museum and asked her to identify an image of Horus. She walked past many possible pictures purporting to be Horus. Instead, she went upstairs and pointed to a small picture in a cabinet that Crowley believed to be genuine. Edith would go on to pronounce that she was not in contact with Horus himself but his messenger Aiwass.

Crowley says that he wrote 'The book of the law' in 3 days between the hours of noon and 1pm. He sat at a desk in the apartment they were staying in, and the voice of Aiwass would come from behind Crowley's left shoulder at the back of the room. He reported the voice as being *"of deep timbre, musical and expressive, its tones, solemn, voluptuous, tender, fierce..."*. The voice was said to have no *"native or foreign accent"*. This is how Crowley claims the book was written.

It is clear from Crowley's life that he, too, was no stranger to myth, and also had a deep love of the occult.

This book would push the idea that there was only the individual and that it was the individual's right to do whatever they wanted. More disturbingly that you should be able to kill anyone who was getting in your way. The strongest should win. It was not explained what happened to the rights of the now-deceased individual. The trouble with Tim's ideas is that in the wrong hands, what was to stop people from agreeing with Aleister Crowley and doing whatever they wanted? To imprint any reality tunnel that enables any egregious action?

We might seek to answer this question with ideas like Law and Morality, but just a cursory look at most Nations and big businesses proves that the leaders of these entities do not operate inside these trifling notions. As I write, Xi Jinping is following what he wants to do in committing Genocide and stamping on anyone he can reach who dares to suggest freedom of thought.

The point stands that we are not looking to just change our internal reality tunnels to suit whatever our ego happens to want in the moment. This, of course, is no change at all. Just a continuation of the same selfish actions we are looking to move away from.

I think in the end, this lack of understanding, in terms of the kind of change we are trying to achieve, combined with the fact that the use of psychedelic drugs can cause psychosis in the wrong person, is still the primary problem with their use in a therapeutic sense. We will also find out later that there are natural and completely safe ways to achieve resolution within the context of unresolved trauma and to achieve psychological change.

When Tim and his colleagues at Harvard started their work with psychedelics, this group of drugs was legal in America.

It wasn't long before concerned parents and staff complained that their sons and daughters were taking drugs and talking about *"dropping out"* – not what they were expecting from an elite educational facility like Harvard. Tim would somewhat inevitably be sacked from Harvard, and the use of psychedelic drugs was made illegal in America for anything other than research – a legal standing that remains in place today.

Tim had been busy, though, travelling America and speaking to as many influential people as he could. He had been to Hollywood and had brought LSD to many parties there. It was even rumoured that John F Kennedy had taken LSD in the White house.

The message was out, and the young of America were listening. It was 1967 and the famous 'summer of love' was about to take place. A commonly quoted statistic was that some seven million Americans took the drug at this time and it quickly became apparent that some people were suffering severe consequences to this sudden mass usage of LSD. If a person had an underlying psychosis, the use of the drug could bring it to the fore. As we now know, we did not see a sudden significant shift in Consciousness, a new balanced world. Instead, we saw neoliberalism's continuing rise, and no psychological evolution transpired in individuals in any significant numbers.

The reasons for this are multiple, but to name two examples: LSD alone is not sufficient to change the world or the individual. We cannot achieve a fundamental change via something external from ourselves. Also, there was, and is, a significant power in the world that did not and does not want a free-thinking population.

Tim would go on to become President Nixon's most wanted man in America and spent many years of his life either in prison or on the run, on dubious charges, only being pardoned when he was no longer a relevant factor to American politics at large.

America had moved on around him. He died in May 1966, having lived the rest of his life in California. A month after his death, the author Robert Anton Wilson received an email:

Dear Robert,

How are you doing? I'm doing fine over here, but it's not what I expected. Too crowded.

Love,

Tim

It was sent from Tim's email account, and no one who had access has ever admitted to sending it.

Fundamentally Tim was a person with a giant intellect and an enormous Ego and did not, in the end, believe that Consciousness had anywhere further to go than the brain. There is no evidence, other than in Spain, that he ever knowingly moved past thinking. His observations and ideas, though, have considerable merit and are well worth your investigation.

Chapter Four

Individualism, Neo-Liberalism, and Shock Doctrine

Up until now I have chosen to write this book through people's stories. Facts and concepts outside the realm of life and people is to see the world without love or beauty and are ultimately of no real consequence.

What we will explore in this chapter is exactly that, ideas devoid of humanity, love, and beauty. This is the story of thinking born of fear and separation from the whole, of greed and the need to dominate others. The primary trouble with thinking when in relationship, as we will see, is it is born of the individual, not of love.

It is fun to tell how Aleister Crowley came to write 'The book of the law' at the beginning of the 20th century, which was the period of time that these ideas of individualism were really accepted into the common narrative. These concepts and actions have been present since time immemorial. It was not started with Alistair Crowley, Friedrich Hayek, or Milton Friedman.

The fun stops abruptly as we see the damage and destruction these ideas have bought about. Hayek and Friedman put forward the idea that economics is subject to the same Intelligence and order that imbues the natural world. Of course, this is ridiculous as economics are purely a product of thinking and have no link to nature or order.

We can look back at religious wars, kingdoms, Dictatorships, and Empires to see how individuals wanting to dominate and control others for their own ends has always been a part of human life. We have evolved in every way other than inwardly, psychologically. Here we are essentially still precisely the same as we always were regarding how we relate to the world and others. We just have more technical knowledge now, which we can apply to the same processes of domination, greed, and environmental destruction.

Due to what has become resignation and apathy in us as a species, we accept this insane world with all its misplaced dogma and ideology, passively accepting its effects on our lives, relationships, passions, and environment. If you have any doubt about this, look now online at what an exploding hydrogen bomb looks like. In this ultimate example of the debasement of nature, as we watch the hydrogen atoms tearing apart, we see vividly what we are, what we have become. We take Einstein's brilliant and beautiful theories and use them to tear apart the very fabric of the universe in order to kill, dominate, and control.

Neo-liberalism is the dominant philosophy of our time and essentially stands for profit over people and everything else. A small handful of private interests are allowed to control human and natural life as much as possible, to maximise their profits while taking no responsibility and not giving anything back.

We need to stand back here before we go on and clearly see that money is a man-made law. It is not naturally occurring. To tear our lives apart and destroy our environment based on a man-made construct that can take any shape we wish it to is obviously insane. For many decades now, any connection money had to reality is long gone. It is held together purely because we all buy into the concepts within it.

Regarding neoliberalism, the private interests we are referring to are a few extremely wealthy investors and less than one thousand giant corporations. This group is known as the "Washington consensus". Margaret Thatcher, who was voted into power in the U.K. when I was only 2 years old, and Ronald Reagan, voted in 2 years later, are generally attributed with bringing neo-liberalist ideology into political dominance. Although they were not new ideas and really stem from Friedrich Hayek and Milton Friedman, their neo-liberal ideas fit nicely into the Aleister Crowley fuck you, I am looking after myself school of thinking.

So how is this obviously ridiculous ideology so dominant in our world? Where you are when you read this will determine whether neoliberalism is sold to you via propaganda, shock doctrine, violent repression, cultural conditioning, or a bit of all of these strategies. We don't need to analyse violent repression to understand it. This strategy will generally occur in the 'Third World Countries' also known as 'western dependents'. Here a small, powerful elite in each country will directly benefit financially from the financial rape of their own people and their nations natural resources for the benefit of themselves and the neo-liberal elite defined earlier. In these countries, we see the same pattern of rapidly increasing extreme poverty, destruction of the local environment, reduced access to good health care and education, and increasing control by criminal organisations.

Noam Chomsky offers a couple of good examples of this in his description of the 'Washington consensus' where he quotes from official government documents in his book, Profit Over People:

"High-level documents describe the primary threat to these interests (neo-liberal interests), particularly in Latin America, as "radical" and "nationalistic regimes" that are responsive to popular pressures for "immediate improvement in low living standards of the masses"".

Why would anyone want better living conditions? How dare they!

Ideas of making the world better for the majority of people and the natural world are clearly shown here as getting in the way of the interests of the neoliberal elite. Influential planner George Kennan, who was part of the Washington consensus, advised that we should *"Cease to talk about vague and unreal objectives such as human rights, the raising of the living standards, and democratisation"* and must instead *"deal in straight power concepts"* not *"hampered by idealistic slogans"* about *"altruism and world-benefaction"*. This was quoted directly from 'the secret record'.

The Washington consensus would overthrow Guatemala's first democratic government in 1954 for *"stability"* security for *"the upper classes and large foreign enterprises,"* whose welfare must be preserved. As we are learning, the world's welfare was, and is, of no concern to the Washington consensus. Similar acts by the Washington consensus have been carried out on Chile, Argentina, Brazil, Mexico, Russia and Columbia, to name a few. Afterwards, through changes in law, trade agreements, foreign ownership of businesses, natural resources and banks, these countries are held prisoners forever in this way.

America is the primary aggressor in the neo-liberal movement and is outside of any formal control, whether in law or via force. It is essential to point out that Britain and other European Countries were committing the same atrocities hundreds of years prior to America around the world. A good example of this was when the British blocked Egypt's attempts at economic independence by force on the grounds that *"Britain would not tolerate independent development in that region."*

We are, of course, not talking about the American people as the main aggressors, but this small group of wealthy investors and giant corporations hiding behind the American state (the Washington consensus).

Like every other western population, the average American also has, as a result of Neo-liberalism, seen employment rights and employment contracts change negatively. Average wages have stagnated and shrunk in real terms to the level of the 1950s. Most Americans are only a minute away from losing their jobs if their employer is not happy. There are very few employment rights, and this fear lies at the heart of the American economy. Growth surprisingly to most, is also extremely slow. This significant shift in wealth is known as 'The great divergence'. We have, to some extent, adapted to this reality with increasing personal debt. Both partners working now being the norm, and a rise in capital, like house prices, if you are lucky enough to have any.

War, violence, and law have pushed this damaging ideology in poorer countries; this is a known strategy put forward by Milton Friedman and his acolytes from the Chicago university he taught at. The ideas behind Friedman's ideology is challenging for a democratic government to implement quickly. However, slowly these ideas are being accepted by individuals in these so-called democracies.

In the '50s, 60s, and early 70s, Chile and Argentina were doing increasingly well using 'Keynesian' economic concepts. The state owned all of the big industries in each country, including its natural resources. The state maintained the prices of essential items needed to live. It prevented any significant foreign ownership of businesses and the movement of money away from the country. In Chile, the elected government of Allende were operating very much in the interests of the majority.

All of this made depressing reading for the Washington consensus. What if too many people realise there is a better way of living? Where will our power base be then?

Milton Friedman's Chicago university offered to educate Chile's economic students for free in 1957, an offer refused by the University of Chile as it was seen for what it was: Neoliberalism's attempt to undermine Chile's more socialist Keynesian economy. Instead, The Chicago university paid to set its self up at Chile's Catholic University, a far less prestigious organisation. Here Milton Freidman and his colleagues worked to educate 100 Chileans in Neoliberalist ideology between 1957 and 1970.

Before Chile's elections in 1971, America used a strategy of holding investment and borrowing to the country as well as creating trade tariffs to try and put financial pressure on the Allende government. This did not work. The population of Chile knew where their bread was buttered and voted Allende in again. At this point the Washington consensus believed it was time to overthrow the democratically voted government. The CIA started to liaise directly with Chile's military through various private organisations. The Chicago boys (As the graduates of Milton Friedman's degree became known) started to write up a new economic strategy to be ready for the upcoming coup. When the coup came, it was quickly followed by two further shocks – torture camps and Friedman's economic policies.

Pinochet's coup took place on September 11 1973. Pinochet had complete control of the country's army, navy, marines, and police. He rolled tanks and army vehicles down Santiago's boulevards accompanied by fighter jets to the government buildings where Allende and his colleagues had gathered. 24 rockets were fired into the building. Allende was killed in the attack and Chileans watched as his body was carried out live on television. This was followed by the arrest of 13,500 civilians. The arrests were made as publicly as possible to spread fear, and the prisoners were taken to the two main football stadia where they were tortured and imprisoned. There were also many public executions.

In the end, Pinochet's junta tortured and imprisoned 40,018 people and killed 3065. This brutality was quickly followed by Friedman's economic trinity of privatisation, deregulation, and cuts to social spending. This translated to all state functions, businesses, and natural resources being sold to foreign investors. The deregulation of laws put in place to protect individual rights and a massive drop in the quality of healthcare, education, and other social care. The only people to benefit were the Washington Consensus and a few individuals connected to the junta. The wealthiest 10 per cent of Chile's population had suddenly become 83 per cent richer.

By 1988, 45 per cent of the population had fallen into poverty. Chile is now one of the most unequal societies in the world. This is a report about Chile, but we know that very similar strategies were used in Argentina, Brazil, Bolivia, Russia, and Iraq, to name a few more.

Do not underestimate what you are dealing with regarding the Washington consensus, which also utilises the IMF and the World Bank to do its dirty work. Any country needing a loan from either institution will be told in no uncertain terms that the country concerned must sign up to Friedman style shock economic doctrine in return. The culture bought forward by the Chicago university is the dominant philosophy of both institutions. They do not accept that the inhabitants of the countries looking for help via loans should have a democratic say on the economic philosophy employed in their own country. Also, once they know a country is on the ropes, they will hold investment and increase trade restrictions until they have no choice but to submit.

So, why do we accept all this in the West? The short answer is faux democracies, where the line between politicians and business is non-existent, where propaganda and cultural conditioning are expertly utilised, and as Aldous Huxley put it, distraction.

Corporations have vast P.R. budgets, and there is a distinct lack of transparency in the decisions made within corporations and governments. The much-heralded 'free press' is, with a few exceptions, owned and controlled by the same neo-liberal elite. This is why Julian Assange of Wiki-Leaks is considered such a threat. What is the difference between what Wiki-leaks has done and a genuinely free press? The level of transparency Wiki-leaks offers is unquestionably in the public's interest.

Interestingly, as I write, a law has been debated here in the U.K. that would make it illegal to print a story based on an unofficial leak – via Wiki-leaks for example – as it would "go against National secrecy" and would result in the journalist responsible being imprisoned. The government have since backtracked a bit as a few genuine journalists noticed and didn't fancy a stint in prison, but it will be bought back at some later date.

The educational system in the West is designed not to teach people how to think for themselves but how to think.

In the U.K., where I live, a governmental organisation called OFSTED keeps a strict eye on teachers to maintain this tick box system. Students who conform sufficiently during their schooling are rewarded with qualifications, better pay, and higher positions in society. When an ideology is so pervasive, it can be tough for someone to see beyond it. It is just accepted as unchangeable and 'normal'. It is also made very clear to us constantly that any deviation from the neo-liberal ideology will end in financial and social catastrophe. Words like 'socialism' and 'communism' are shouted at the mere mention of change towards a fairer system. Fear and education are used expertly to keep you where they need you.

If we look at Friedman's trinity of privatisation, deregulation, and cuts to social spending, we can see, wherever we are living, how these ideas have slid insidiously into our world.

In the U.K., since I was born in 1976, privatisation has been moving at a pace. Under Margaret Thatcher, between 1982 and 1986, Jaguar, British Telecom, Cable and Wireless, British Aerospace, Britoil, and British Gas were privatised. Then, between 1987 and 1991, British Steel, British Petroleum, Rolls Royce, British Airways, and water and electricity utilities were sold. Between 1992 and 1996, British Coal, Powergen, National Power, and National Rail were privatised. Since then, Royal Mail, Parts of the NHS, Schools, Probation, Prisons and roads have been sold, or contracts were given to private businesses.

In terms of deregulation, we see laws changed and challenged that slowly erode our rights. Access to legal representation is slowly made increasingly difficult and more expensive. By taking money out of this area of law, the quality of the representation is also gradually diminishing. The result of all this is now thought of as 'the gig economy'. Basically, companies pay less, offer less, and take less responsibility.

The slow erosion of public spending in the U.K. is ongoing. We can see here without too much research how these ideas are dominant in all our societies. I am sure wherever you are reading this you will see a similar pattern, if not a lot worse!

The central doctrine put forward by neo-liberal groups is shown here in a quote by Robert McChesney found at the beginning of Noam Chomsky's 'Profit over People':

"Neo-liberal initiatives are sold as free-market policies that encourage private enterprise and consumer choice, reward personal responsibility and entrepreneurial initiative, and undermine the dead hand of the incompetent, bureaucratic and parasitic government, that can never do good even if well-intended, which it rarely is."

We'll start with the first claim of a free market. A free market would be a level market, open to any business anywhere, with no restrictions at all to trade. Of course, there is no such thing as a free market; there are laws sensibly in place to restrict child labour, for example. Equally, we wouldn't be able to receive payment for dumping toxic waste in our gardens. These restrictions are put in place for our own benefit. It is also true that not many have the opportunity or finance to start a business.

Another way markets are not free is the massive subsidisation of big corporations through taxpayer money, biased laws, and trade agreements. An extensive study of transnational corporations by Winfried Ruigrock and Rob van Tulder found that *"virtually all of the world's largest core firms have experienced a decisive influence from government policies and/or trade barriers on their strategy and competitive position"*.

The financial crash of 2007 was caused by historic corruption, greed, and irresponsibility in the financial markets. This led to us, the taxpayer, bailing out the entire rotten edifice of the banks and the business world, only to see the wealth of the neo-liberal elite double. Since then, there has been no real change. The claim of a free market is a myth.

The next thing to look at is monopolies. Let us simplify things here to understand them. If there were 10 pizza shops in your local town, each privately owned and operating from similar premises, with similar overheads, the price of the pizzas would be self-regulating, assuming they didn't illegally all meet up and fix a price, (another trick of neo-liberalism). Price would be considered relative to the competition and the individual's subjective opinion on the quality of the pizza or the service from each outlet.

There would be no point in one shop selling pizzas for £100 each when you could find a pizza of comparable quality down the road for £10. This is how balanced competition can create a fairer, more innovative marketplace. Equally, if one shop made terrible pizzas and swore at their customers, they would go out of business pretty quickly. So, competition maintains quality and drives creativity – in this case, via quicker deliveries, new flavours, or better baking styles, maybe? A monopoly would be if one company bought all the shops and then increased prices in all of them while reducing the quality. At this point, as a customer, you have no leverage other than never to buy pizza locally again.

This model would also affect wages. If you were an exceptionally reliable and gifted pizza maker outside of a monopoly, it would be in the pizza shop owner's interest to employ you. Also, the rival shops would like to hire you. Therefore, your employer would have to give you reasonable wages, holiday, sickness cover, etc. Otherwise, the rival shop would be able to convince you to leave and work for them. This is no longer relevant in a monopoly as the need for a quality pizza maker is no longer very important.

When I was younger, monopolies were spoken about regularly in the news, and a monopoly commission in government was charged with, as much as possible, preventing monopolies from forming. Although this department is still present, it is now largely without power. It tends just to rewrite the laws to suit business rather than address the issues created by monopolies. Vast global companies now take the idea of monopolies to new levels driving down wages, growth, entrepreneurialism, and actually taking responsibility away from individuals, the exact opposite of the claims made by neo-liberal dogma.

Interestingly the reason communism was such a failure was that control was limited to a few central bodies, with no accountability or competition. Much like modern global capitalism!

Another claim is that neo-liberalism drives creativity and technological advancement. Let us think about this carefully. Technological advances are present but also diminished by neoliberalism as the company profits are always more important. This restricts the movement of information and prevents intelligent people from working together to make the world a better place.

Let us think of an example. If all the World's scientists were able to work together, free from economic restrictions and in a non-protective transparent way, not in response to what makes money, but to benefit our health and the environment, what could we then achieve?

At the moment, various companies may have half the information necessary to solve many of our problems while other companies have the other half. Neither will speak to the other as they are scared they won't profit sufficiently from it.

Creativity is also present but is always geared towards what makes money, not how to re-imagine the world for the better.

Another example might be that as washing detergent is such a massive way for big corporations to make a profit, many gifted scientists are spending their lives looking at ways to improve how we clean clothes rather than how the world works and how we might live more harmoniously within it. In the end, the focus of scientific study is purely directed at what makes the most money.

Neo-liberalism is, as we have shown, the opposite of democracy.

America is now entirely governed in the interests of the wealthy elite. They have lobbying, where individuals and corporations openly pay government members to speak to them and explain what they want them to do. The American political system is described by many as an oligarchy!

The other tactic that we see in the American system is people taking high up political roles only to resign and take up a post in a private company. They then use their connections within the government to push their personal agender for personal and corporate profit. Here we see no genuine separation between public-serving political or civil roles and private corporations. Equally, via the 'free press', anyone the neo-liberal elite considers a threat is discredited and ridiculed to prevent them from gaining significant public support.

Likewise, any narrative that is seen to push the agenda of politicians and business is constantly rolled out in countless articles and made to seem like the only sensible option. This system of lobbying and biased journalism is similar in all western countries, although not always so openly as in America.

You cannot have a true democracy with neo-liberalism; they are directly opposed to each other. One is looking for everyone to live in a fair society, and one is designed in the interests of a tiny majority. Again, this reminds us of what occurred in communist systems.

It is ultimately true that, if properly united, we as a human race wouldn't even need to shout to change all this. We are the 'ultimate weapon' against neo-liberalism. If only we were united enough, we could calmly say that's enough of that thank you, it's time you went home. A small group of people cannot rule over a large one forever if the large group does not recognise their authority.

All of the claims of neo-liberalism are lies and misdirection. It's a small group of wealthy investors and corporations operating to harm you and your family and your environment purely for their own benefit and profit.

The Fundamental dogma put forward by neo-liberalism does not need to be in this world at all. In fact, if it continues, there won't be a world habitable to humans before long. We can change it. Not through other ideologies or concepts, not by force, but by changing ourselves inwardly and seeing and connecting to each other and our humanity again in its purest form, which is wholeness.

Apart from the natural world, nothing about the world we live in is a given. It didn't need to look like this. The world we inhabit has been created by our thinking, and it can always change again.

Nothing in the universe is not moving and changing constantly. Life is movement. Life is change.

I have picked specific examples and bits of history here to illustrate neo-liberalism and its effects. Please don't take my word for any of this. Look it up for yourself. It is essential to understand the world as it is to understand where we are as a species. If you don't know where the power lies and what forms that takes, you can't understand it or hope to change it.

Technology has moved globalisation on rapidly. The control imposed by corporations is moving fast, and the loss of personal control over your life and mine at this point is significant. Look for yourself. Please.

The above economic picture serves as an example of what happens when we let a group of psychologically under evolved people have too much power and control. What all these people have in common is that they cannot see past their own reality tunnels and gigantic egos, as a consequence of this, they suffer from insatiable greed born of fear.

Chapter Five

A world in which ideas do not exist

If we want to make a genuine and radical change in ourselves and open up the possibility of radical change in the World, it is essential we understand that we cannot make these changes within the landscape of thinking. These changes cannot occur through the application of knowledge, law, scientific models, ideology or force. Why is this? Let us come back to our friend Jiddu Krishnamurti and see if his ideas can throw any light on this question.

In answer to our original question, 'What is thinking?' Krishnamurti would say that *"consciousness is its contents."* What does he mean by this? We can say for sure that thinking takes place in the brain, that this process takes place in time, that it is a physical, material process.

As a newborn child, as our senses develop, we begin to take in the World around us through them. The brain is, in the end, situated in the head. It can only experience the World through our senses, not directly as it floats in the darkness of the human cranium. This means that, while in thinking, our interpretation of the World is always limited to how our senses perceive the Universe around us and how the brain interprets the incoming information.

As we grow and our senses and brains establish themselves we fill the mind with many experiences. Or, in fact, how we have interpreted and remembered these experiences.

We fill our minds with experiences and knowledge we have collected directly and indirectly. We take in our families, different cultures, the people that live and work around us, all the way out to the whole World and on into the Universe – if we choose to take any notice!

We take in religions, ideologies, concepts, political and economic structures, social rules and norms, and social structures. We read books, watch television, films, and any number of formats online. We listen to music, go on social media etc., etc....

We listen to the ideas and opinions of our families, our teachers, the media, politicians, celebrities, friends of course and anyone else we come across that cares to give them. We go to school at a young age and are educated in any number of subjects and are told what is and isn't important to know about. As a result, we form definitive ideas about ourselves based on all of this collected information. We continuously label ourselves: I am not funny, I am funny, I am not good looking, I am good looking, etc., and we form similar opinions about others in the same way.

We interpret all of this and many more pieces of information, and we store them, memorise them in the brain. This process of filling our consciousness is limited by our senses, the capacity of the brain, what we have encountered and what we choose to take notice of. To mention just a few limiting factors.

It is also important to note that our memories are far from perfect and that these memories will change over time. If 5 people were to go on the same night out at a restaurant, they would all form different memories of the same experience. They would have had different food, different conversations, and different emotional reactions. Their attention will have been drawn to different things. If you were to interview all of them about the evening the following morning, then again a year later, their memories of the event would differ again. It does us no harm to remind ourselves of the tenuous link between our memories, consciousness, and reality. We then generally live within these ideas, opinions and memories as if they were infallible truths.

Imagine filling up our consciousness all the time with all this information and how we have interpreted it. This is the contents of our consciousness and also the extent of it. This is what Krishnamurti means by *"consciousness is its contents"*. As we know, all of that information, as great and as broad as it may be in some people, comes nowhere even close to knowing everything. This is indisputable.

We can say then that the contents of my consciousness, the foundation of my thinking and actions, is fragmented. It is lots of tiny fragments of information with many, many, many gaps. We can also say that consciousness represents the past, what has gone before, memories. We can say then that thinking is the bringing back of the past, brought to bear in the now.

To continue our observations, we can point out that thinking is static in its nature. It struggles with discovering anything new as it can only view things from the perspective of what has gone before. Thinking is limited to the parameters of its contents. I am only capable of thinking within my experience. Another important observation is that thinking is inherently reductionistic in its nature. This means that instead of seeing the big picture, the Whole, the mind breaks every subject down into non-dynamic pieces to attain an incomplete understanding of the subject and build models of thought around the subject.

We are told that if only we just had enough knowledge, then thinking would be sufficient to solve all our problems. That we would be the gods of all we survey. Our investigation of thinking, thus far, quickly proves this assertion to be false. It is just not possible. Physics tells us that even if we were able to document everything happening in the Universe, it would still not become predictable.

Thinking is not truth. It can only produce some instrumental models and observations to help explain ourselves and the Universe around us. These models are of considerable value, but only if we view them for what they are – different models of thought that are useful in certain situations, knowing all the time that they are not the complete truth.

Robert Anton Wilson coined the term 'multiple model agnosticism' to highlight this point. We will look at this in more detail later.

Jiddu Krishnamurti did not stop here in his discussions around consciousness. Bear with me here; there is a lot to get through, but I can assure you it's all worth listening to.

His next important observation is that thinking creates a centre. In this case, we become centred around our minds, around the Ego. When you centre yourself around a fixed point, you inadvertently separate yourself from the Whole and create a finite border around yourself, creating a defined space in relation to everything and everyone else. This assertion that we are separated, different, unrelated individuals is a central belief in the World. It is found in every aspect of our lives. It is a central tenet of the conditioning we experience.

When we divide the World up like this (which is, as we have said, the nature of thinking) we create dualities and inevitably end up in a state of conflict, where we are in constant competition with each other.

In the landscape of thinking we perceive the World through the Ego. The Ego is constantly striving to become something, as it is based in the idea of survival. We don't except what we already are – ourselves.

What is even stranger for us to understand is that this constant need to become something, which occurs over a period of time, is ultimately a selfish act. This is because it is always viewed from the individual's perspective, the wish to be better and therefore more successful or powerful relative to others.

Within the context of the Ego, we are always looking for recognition and a pat on the back, for others to recognise our brilliance. The flip side of this is that we are constantly comparing ourselves to others. When we compare ourselves with other people we begin to form judgements, which pulls us away from our true nature. We begin to imitate others rather than being ourselves. We have no inherent value if we are not ourselves. To become an imitation of something or someone is a waste of your life. It constitutes a massive loss of potential, and you will get lost. This, in turn, will significantly affect your Health.

The ideas and fears formed around the illusion of being fundamentally separate from everyone else are a significant cause of our anxieties and unhappiness. All of you reading this will know the feeling of emotional pain, loneliness, confusion, and sadness. When we really stop and look, we find that we are in an almost perpetual state of discontentment. We look inside ourselves and are not content with what we see, then we look at the World outside of ourselves and are also discontented with what we see. It is quite a thing to realise that, in the landscape of thinking, we are living in a constant state of varying discontentment. Just stop and let this sink in for a second.

We are told then of God, of religion, of a third entity; and through the landscape of thinking, we look at all these ideas and cannot help but build images, ideology, opinions, and dogma. We miss what is because, again, we are lost in what we have imagined. This leads us to more disorder and conflict – this time around the things we have imagined about religion and God. We are incapable, while still in the landscape of thinking, of resolving any of this.

Another possible course of action, if we don't wish to become embroiled in divine ideas, is to disassociate. Many addictions form within the attempt to disassociate, especially as we often don't even realise we are actively separating from ourselves.

As always in life, there are two sides of every coin, opposites, yin and yang. With that perspective, let's look at the positive aspects of thinking. Thinking from a technical standpoint is not only important, it is essential. I would not be able to write this without thinking. You would not be able to read it. Technically, thinking could not be more vital to our existence. Thinking has brought about communication, mathematics, physics, music, dancing, art, medicine, cars, flight, computers, and the internet. The list is magnificent and vast.

Our technical evolution is astounding and constantly ongoing. The opposite side of this coin means that thinking has also brought about the nuclear bomb, war, division, the idea of nation, slavery, the destruction of the natural World, crime, neoliberalism, repression, racism, and misogyny. This list goes on and on too. Our psychological evolution has, in essence, been non-existent and has not kept up with our technical development. This is a huge issue because it does not bode well when you combine our level of technical knowledge with our stunted psychological growth.

When I see the recent stories of UFO sightings by the American Military suggesting technological knowledge well beyond our present understanding, we have to infer that any society that has evolved technically to this point without destroying themselves implies that they must also have evolved psychologically. Therefore, we can also conclude that, whoever it is, they should not be feared.

As I have said previously, our friend Krishnamurti looked at consciousness and its effects from many different angles. Our next look into this is his comment that *"thinking destroys relationship"*; and the other big one is the origins of fear. And no, it's not Aliens!

I am going to ask you at this juncture to think about someone close to you. It could be your partner, a sibling, a parent, a child, or a friend. As you bring this person to mind, it is likely that several thoughts, images, and ideas come forward. These thoughts, images, and ideas will be the product, as we have learned, of memories, assumptions, and ideas you have built up around this person. They will be based on previous encounters, stories you have been told about them, and how your brain has interpreted this information.

We do not necessarily realise how these thoughts, images, and ideas get between ourselves and anyone with whom we are in a relationship. This includes the relationship we have with ourselves.

To give you an example, before you meet and while you meet this person: all the ideas, images and thoughts you have about them will sit between you and them. You will have ideas, and thoughts about how they speak, think, look, behave, and act. You will make assumptions about what will happen within your encounter, how you will respond and feel etc.

Suppose we follow this line of enquiry to its end. In that case, we find that you are not genuinely in a relationship with this person very often, if at all. We realise all that is happening is that your thoughts, images, and ideas are meeting this person, and probably the same is true for them too. All this baggage is getting between you and them and preventing you from really relating fully in the now. It is possible to drop all of this and to relate properly in the moment. In this way, the relationship is genuine and not static, and the new can constantly manifest. We can be free of all the constant analysis and imagery that tends to define most human relationships.

It is daunting to suddenly see how often we have not been in genuine relationships with our loved ones and ourselves – that lives have sometimes come and gone without us ever having truly been in relationship with each other! Instead, we come to see that we have been completely caught up in the images, words, and analysis created in the brain. The word 'Mum' is not the person. The images you have of your Mum are equally not the person. It is not a complete image of her, not the whole truth of that person. Then we see with a shock that thought has robbed us of a genuine relationship with even our own Mother. This is what Krishnamurti means when he say's *"Thinking is the death of relationship"*!

Another typical example of this juxtaposition between a genuine relationship and one based only in our thinking is when we fancy someone.

When I was younger, David Beckham was a source of a lot of interest from boys and girls alike. He is a good-looking man, and it was thought that because he didn't speak much (Due to a lack of confidence) whatever narrative people had created around him in their minds was never significantly challenged. In essence, they could superimpose any character type they wanted and create what they felt to be the perfect person for them.

We are all open to this kind of illusion around other people. We ignore the real person and just create them in our own image and then fall in love with, or dislike, this imagined image. How many relationships take place like this?

What do we do now, then? With no better ideas, we generally turn to thinking to try and resolve all the disorder in our relationships and all around us. We try thinking in the form of science, psychology, philosophy, ideology, religion, politics, laws, etc. But, and for me, this brings us to a fundamental question: Is it possible to bring about order through thinking?

The Universe is in a constant state of dynamic order around us, whether we are aware of this or not. The Earth continues to rotate while revolving around the Sun. The Sun, in turn, continues to revolve around the milky way and so on, and so on. From our perspective here on Earth, the Sun comes up and goes down. Tides rise and fall. Seasons come and go. The many occupants of this planet are in their own loop of life and death. Everything is in constant movement.

The Earth is believed to be over 4.5 billion years old, and life began here with single-cell organisms, bacteria and archaea, about 4 billion years ago. We do not know how or why life suddenly manifested itself, although obviously, there are theories. We do know that bacteria are evolving at a dizzying rate relative to ourselves. What takes a human 20 to 40 years to achieve, to multiply, takes a bacterium only 20 minutes. To put it into context, this evolution was happily moving along for about 3.7 billion years before Homo Sapiens is thought to have evolved into existence. That is the constant evolution of multiple bacteria and archaea every 20 minutes for now 4 billion years!

Somewhere within this process occurred the most significant jump in evolution the Earth has ever seen – an occurrence so unlikely it has never happened again in the 2.7 billion years since the evolution of the eukaryote cell is thought to have occurred. What happened, it is believed, was that a bacteria cell was swallowed by an archaea cell and formed a symbiotic relationship leading to the origin cell of complex life – what we and every other example of complex life are formed from. These cells, in brief, have mitochondria, where energy is created, microtubules and a nucleus are all contained within an outer wall. All of this evolution happened long before we theorised about its origins and pondered the start of complex life.

Still, today single-cell organisms of varying sizes, shapes, and functions are in a constant state of movement, evolution, multiplication, and death. We also now know that bacteria can happily and efficiently borrow DNA from each other as required in a process called 'horizontal gene transfer'. This means they can evolve instantly without multiplying if this is feasible, and it is desirable to do so. This process happens only when they are close to each other.

All this dynamic order is happening without us being aware of it necessarily, and certainly without us having to control it. We have evolved around and through bacteria and archaea and depend on them for our continued existence in a multitude of ways. Most of us do not live within this reality and happily spend our lives trying to kill as many as possible as often as possible, failing to understand that the more diverse a number of bacteria present in a given place, the better the balance, the better the overall Health. So, by killing 99.9% in any given area, we actually form a black hole for any bacteria, good or bad, to thrive without competition – an example of us attempting to control what happens around us within this order and actually just making things worse, creating disorder from order.

If we zoom in a little more, we go past single cells to see the World instead from the perspective of atoms and molecules. Here we enter another view of the Whole, again in a constant state of movement, all inter-connected with everything else in the Universe. Whether we look at the Universe from the perspective of the planets or from the perspective of atoms, we're viewing the same whole from yet another different place, all as real and as relevant as each other. Imagine ourselves shrinking enough to see an atom so it appeared to us as the exact size of St Pauls Cathedral. The nucleus would be roughly the size of a cricket ball. The electrons would be like fly's buzzing around the outside. What would make up the rest? Space. Nothingness. If we were to look at molecules, we would see a vast amount of space between the atoms. So much nothingness. In fact, if we were to collect all the actual matter from every human on the Earth and compress it together in one place, it would be the size of a sugar cube. A sugar cube!

If we continue to increase our magnified view, as we might when using Google maps, consider what the Universe would look like if we could shrink ourselves down to view the sub-atomic World. What happens here regarding sub-atomic particles and time etc., the World of quantum gravity and mechanics? Here we leave the predictable Universe we imagine existing in our minds far behind. Nothing here is predictable or mechanical and it's impossible to view any of it without changing what we are looking at. After all, we are a part of what we are looking at. This landscape is not separate from ours. We are just looking at the same movement from yet another perspective. The quantum World is best viewed as an endless series of events.

It is safe to say we are only at the beginning when understanding the quantum landscape, and many amazing theories are out there. Few are agreed upon but Heisenberg, Bohr, and Schrodinger have created amazing working models of this landscape. It is shown to be strange, unpredictable, and unintuitive to our thinking. It has undoubtedly challenged a lot of previous models of thought.

As we make our way through these different ways of viewing our World, it starts to dawn on us that the movement of the Whole and the natural order within is so dizzyingly complex and vast that our brains start to ache just trying to grasp it. Once you really see this, understand its truth fully. The attempt to dominate and force change on this beautiful and perfectly ordered movement through reductionistic models and selfish desires appears to be misplaced. To be diplomatic about it. The nature of seeing things in a reductionistic way is that we focus only on a tiny part of this whole movement without considering how it works in context with everything else.

We certainly are capable of making changes within this reductionistic viewpoint. These changes can look pretty good initially, but we often fail to appreciate that these changes, applied from thinking and not from within Intelligence with a capital I, set off a series of unfathomable events that ripple through the Whole – producing in the end ever greater levels of disorder.

This is what we are coming to understand now about the ecological change cascading all around us. We are in what is described as the 'sixth great extinction', our soil is being decimated by industrial farming, and the Earth's weather systems are changing in ever more unpredictable and dramatic ways. Order cannot and will never be achieved through our thinking. Order happens outside of thought, not within it! Again, let this sink in. What do you think about that?

Suppose we wanted to try and interpret this interconnected Wholeness from the perspective of thinking when considering ourselves and our Health. In that case, we might ask ourselves: What is happening in me right now? We could start with examining our skin, the multitudes of our own cells, the bacteria, viruses, mites, etc., that live here, and how these differ from place to place. For example, we share only 6 % of the bacteria found on the palm of one hand compared with the other. The exact conditions, tissue types and functions in different body areas create entirely different environments.

This is all in a constant state of change as you get on with your day-to-day life. We would also have to measure and examine what is happening in your bones, nervous system, endocrine system, lymphatic system, immune system, cardiovascular system, interstitial fluids, fascia, ligaments, muscles, finger and toenails, hair, meninges, oesophagus, stomach, small intestine, large intestine, pancreas, gall bladder, appendix, nose, and ears to name a few. We would have to investigate every cell and what was happening within, how they were communicating with each other – look at every gene, protein, and enzyme.

All of this will also be in a constant state of movement and change. The bacteria will fluctuate between balance and dysbiosis. You will be rested or tired, hungry or full, exercising or asleep. How long ago was it you had a good night's sleep? Are you eating good food? Are you absorbing the food properly?

When did you last fight off a virus? What traumas have you experienced in your life? Are these resolved? Where are you regarding your natural development physically and spiritually? What do you think about all this?

This gives us a small taste of how complex and dynamic we are, even if we could, by some miracle, measure and quantify all of the above information. Which is still not the Whole. In the time it would take us to process it all and interpret it, everything would have changed again. That information would have lost most of its relevance. Are you still confident that an external person can know exactly what is happening regarding yourself through their thinking? Are you really confident about that last diagnosis? They are partially right sometimes, sometimes not even that.

It is not a big jump from here to see how these reductionistic views could lead to treatments, and even operations, that make us decidedly worse than we were before.

Science has come to mean 'to measure'. And therefore, it is the attempt to measure what is measurable within this vastly complex, dynamic, unpredictable interconnected movement we call the Universe. Wholeness.

As I have clearly stated, there is considerable value in a scientific viewpoint. Still, it has very definitive parameters and is by definition a static view of a dynamic universe or person. Science itself sits in the landscape of thought and thinking. Therefore, it is also a view of this information from the perspective of whoever is looking. Science, in the end, is a sea of information. It has no opinion. It is we who interpret this information and decide what it means and how to respond to it. It has value, but that value has parameters.

Suppose we continue to only view and manipulate the World around us from this perspective. In that case, there is only one outcome – continued and greater levels of disorder. The next time you hear someone say in a debate, "well, it's not scientific", with a negative inference, think about this chapter and ask yourself whether there is another way to view what they are talking about. Is it fair to write off everything outside of what is measurable? We have learnt that Health and order are brought about naturally outside of thinking. It is not the height of intelligence to ignore Wholeness.

This also brings us to ask: why are we always trying to control everything anyway? The origin of this need to control is fear, but what are the roots of fear itself? Krishnamurti would say that the fundamental cause of fear is *"psychological time"*. To find out what he means by this, we must first ask what is psychological time, and what connects it to fear?

We understand what we mean by watch time and calendar time, which links to the movements of the Earth relative to the Sun. Also, we know the time it takes us to drive to work or to a particular destination. All this is known collectively as chronological time.

Psychological time refers to being afraid of something that we imagine will happen in the future or remembering something that has happened in the past that we do not want to be repeated. We have many thoughts and images around fear of the future and what has happened in the past.

Another example would be the ideas, thoughts, and images we have around self-improvement. I think today I am not knowledgeable enough to do this job, but I hope in the future I will be, and I am fearful of that not coming true. I can worry about not being good enough to achieve all kinds of things.

It helps if we accept I am what I am and that everyone has been given different skills and passions. If I understand that, it takes no time to be myself now, that things will naturally unfold. If you follow your heart, not your mind, you will find out what these gifts are for yourself. If I remain with this natural unfolding as it chooses to present, without wanting to change it, then for me there is no psychological time. I accept, embrace, and value what is.

We create psychological time in our minds when we are caught in the illusion of being separate, unrelated individuals, when we are not aware of the whole that we are a part of. This is possibly the most challenging step to trust in Wholeness and the implicit order within and just let go. Here is a Taoist fable written by Chung Tzu that sums up beautifully what we need to do:

"Man is born in Tao.

Fishes are born in water Man is born in Tao.

If fishes, born in water,

seek the deep shadow of pond and pool,

all their needs are satisfied.

If man, born in Tao,

sinks into the deep shadow of non-action.

To forget aggression and concern,

he lacks nothing. His life is secure.

Moral: All the fish needs is to get lost in water. All man needs is to get lost in Tao."

Prior to finding this landscape for myself, my life felt a lot like I was being bundled down a raging river with me desperately swimming in various directions trying not to be crushed against various different boulders. Sound familiar? Now life feels more like I am being moved along a steady and calm river, and there are no boulders. Every now and then I think, shouldn't I be swimming and splash about for a bit before remembering that, no, I don't need to, that I am following the natural current? The key is to do the things you love, that bring you joy, and you have a passion for. Then employ those skills to be of service to the World.

When we take the time to look. We see that almost every person in the World is only experiencing their lives from the perspective of thinking. Therefore, they are in a constant state of fear to a greater or lesser degree. We fear death, punishment, control, pain, the dark, spiders, losing our job, losing a friend, partner, or family member. We fear not having enough money or power or having another person in a position of power over us.

Krishnamurti looked in detail at the different facets of fear: death, comparison, seeking security, desire, thought, and psychological time. Fear robs us of our freedom and of Intelligence with a capital I; and more importantly, it robs us of Love. Where there is fear, there is no Love. Fear limits our lives. It is the root of many heinous actions and non-actions. It is the root of hate, and it allows you to be easily manipulated and controlled.

Krishnamurti would be at pains to explain that the answer to this is not to deny we are fearful. He would tell you to sit with it, see it, feel it, know it. Once we see the truth of something, we change, then Intelligence with a capital I, that does not take place in the landscape of thought, can enter. Below I have gone through the different facets of fear as perceived by Krishnamurti:

Comparison: We are constantly compared to and comparing ourselves with others. It is so constant, and every day you can be forgiven for thinking, "what is wrong with it?". We are compared with others at home, at school, at work, when playing games, and most commonly now online via social media.

Within this constant comparison, we are always viewed positively or negatively for many reasons, all contained within thinking. We now know how biased that is. In the digital age, we are becoming even more desperate for approval if this is possible! We want others to agree with us, to like us, to admire us. The trouble is that comparison is a facet of fear. We are fearful we are not clever enough, not funny enough, not successful enough, not wealthy enough, not good looking enough. Comparison is therefore intimately bound up in feelings of shame.

Shame is an extremely powerful emotion and should never be underestimated. Its effects are profound. Shame has been shown many times in studies to be a driving force behind negative behaviour and negative thoughts. We are desperate to avoid facing it, and it will make you ill.

The other side of comparison is if I compare myself to you. I might feel that relatively speaking, you are more interesting, more intelligent, more articulate, more likeable. This, in turn, leads me to start imitating you and others instead of being myself. Eventually, in the end, if we are not careful, this will lead to me losing myself completely.

To quote Krishnamurti: *"We become second-hand humans, mere imitations of ourselves."* I am always saying to my two daughters, *"If you're not yourself, who are you?"* to which they answer, admittedly in a bored monotone, *"Nobody"*. Even within their apparent indifference, they understand the truth of this. We will look at the effects of losing yourself in more detail in the book. It has many implications regarding our Health, both physically and emotionally. For now, we can say comparison, which is endemic in society, is a source of fear.

Seeking security: We don't need to carefully explore the link here to understand how the need for security links with fear. We seek security inwardly in ourselves and outwardly in the World around us. Having shelter is a fundamental need and essential if we are to feel secure. We need a roof over our heads to be dry and warm or cool. We need clean water, and clean air, and healthy food. We also need shelter from the violence of the World, especially as children.

The trouble is we take this need for security way too far and don't consider, or maybe care, that others have the same needs. Within this, our search for shelter becomes competitive and utterly entrenched in fear. We look for security in the idea of nation, for example, and we imagine what will happen in the future if we don't act to defend ourselves.

Within these ideas and images, we move away from our humanity. We begin to see people born on the other side of an arbitrary line drawn on a map as being less worthy of basic security, shelter, water, and food than we are. Within this fear, we condemn millions to a life of violence, poverty, and misery.

Another place in which we seek security and shelter is maybe more surprising. This is knowledge, something which, as we have learnt, we often overestimate. We accumulate knowledge often only to advance our personal standing, wealth, and power in society. We then attempt to make knowledge exclusive. We are told our whole existence depends on the accumulation of knowledge, an assumption that all our schools and universities have at their hearts -- as is exclusivity! It is not easy to access top educational institutions.

Another common place people seek security is in religion and especially religious dogma. If I just follow these rules, I will go to heaven or paradise, be re-incarnated, etc.... We build in our mind's eye images around the idea of God and the divine. Often God is seen in a patriarchal form, for example. These images and thoughts are created in the brain via thinking, and we end up in the ridiculous position of praying to images and ideas of our own making, literally praying to an illusion of our own design.

We do this because we see the chaos inside us, see it outside of us, and we are scared. We want something to change, but we don't know how to bring it about. We want something outside of the natural World and outside of ourselves, a third party, to save us, without us having to change.

I am not saying there is no supernatural Intelligence beyond the mind. I am just challenging the dogma, images, and thinking we create around religion and the divine.

We look for security in the same way in our relationships. We find ourselves thinking if I am in a relationship with this person, everything will be ok. My life will fall into place, and therefore I won't need to change. Or we build relationships whereby our destructive behaviours are considered normal. If we are both constantly drunk all the time, we can frame it as being perfectly normal.

Relationships like this where we depend on someone else to bring about change for us or support our bad life choices are known as co-dependent relationships. The big problem with these relationships is that we remain unchanged, but now we are terrified of the other person leaving! This fear of being rejected is the seed of all kinds of controlling, abusive, and violent relationships.

The idea of nation sits in this need for security. Nation ultimately is a grandiose form of tribalism. The lines that we draw around nations are not imprinted on the ground. They only exist in our thinking. Even the island I live on, here in the U.K., is divided up into Scotland, England and Wales.

From here are decided the rights and fates of people living within these imaginary, arbitrary lines. We understand that where you are born in the World will largely dictate the fabric of your life. We seem to accept the notion that the fate of people within our own nation is immensely more important than the fate of those living outside of it. For example, with the COVID 19 virus, we see that most people seem to care significantly more if people are dying inside their own country than they do for those outside of it. The virus has also shown up the obvious wealth discrepancies between and within nations.

During a recent political campaign here in the U.K, linked to whether we should leave the European Union, Nigel Farage proudly stood in front of a picture showing Syrian refugees trying to escape the war there. They were trying to find shelter for themselves and their families. He did not care about their fate and wasn't looking to help them. Instead, he was garnering support for a more nationalist agenda of keeping them out of the U.K., inviting us to infer that refugees and foreign nationals are the seed of all our problems.

These ideas are increasingly popular in the World. They are the product of fear through the seeking of security on the one hand and the Machiavellian use of our fear to further a political agenda on the other. People can be very caring in certain aspects of their lives, and at the same time, very uncaring in others. They might, for example, obsess about how the coronavirus is going to affect themselves and those around them while letting others die of without giving it a thought.

As we have learnt, this fear is continued into economic philosophies like neo-liberalism. Whereby certain countries, and more specifically individuals within specific countries, are more than happy to profit off the back of the suppression and death of others, as long as they are ok. Business has long profited from the sale of arms and from war, for example. It also benefits from your fears, and more specifically, your reaction to fear. The irony is that the wealthy elite themselves are not immune to fear, and in fact, are often acting entirely from fear. It has always made me laugh to think of all those millionaires and billionaires crowded into tiny tax-free areas like Monaco, so they don't have to pay tax. So they can hide away from the rest of the World. They are very wealthy but still limited by fear. Still hiding away like little mice.

Again, we are not looking to pretend this fear does not exist. As we said earlier, to see the truth of fear and its effects we need to see it and feel it in ourselves – to see the truth behind its effect on our thinking, how it divides us.

Then Intelligence comes into play; once something is seen and understood for what it is, it can be changed.

Division by nations, religions, and races happens only in our own minds. None of it is necessary. We are all human beings, living on one World.

Desire: this is a subtle column of fear. We cannot suppress desire as is often preached in various religions and societies. We are best served by understanding it instead.

The whole economic world ticks to the beat of desire. You need to be wealthier, have a bigger house, a better car and nicer clothes. If you don't, you appear to be a loser.

Desire can also obviously be sexual; this is further complicated in the modern World by easy access to online pornography and dating sites.

Think about something or someone you desire now. Feel it without analysing it. What does it feel like? How does your body experience it? If we think we shouldn't desire sex or material objects, that is a thought process. One part of your consciousness is looking at another part and trying to dominate or change it. This creates internal conflict and divides you into an observer and the observed. They are both you! This, unfortunately, mimics a lot of modern-day mindfulness training.

If I notice beauty, a beautiful sunset, a beautiful person, or a beautiful object, this happens outside of thought and is spontaneous. Very quickly, though, after we notice beauty, a thought will arrive. Beauty quickly then turns into desire. Desire to see that sunset again, to own that car, to be with that person. This is the difference between beauty and desire.

Here is our old friend fear again. Fear that we cannot have what we desire or that someone else will gain what we desire. Don't try to change this. Just see it as it happens. See if you can notice the moment you drift away from beauty and into desire. See the truth of it.

A further insight into the effects of thinking on the mind came from a study conducted by Richard Davidson in 2002 at the University of Wisconsin-Madison.

In conjunction with the Dalai Lama, a number of Buddhist monks (who are very experienced meditators) visited Wisconsin University and had their brain waves looked at via an EEG while meditating and not meditating.

In people who are not experienced meditators, a particular type of brain wave called Gamma waves has been noticed for about half a second after you solve a problem – or bite into an apple, for example. These gamma waves are very hard to see on EEGs, and it often takes days to filter out gamma waves relative to the other brain waves so they can be seen. In the Buddhist Monks, though, this brain wave was always present to a level perceptible immediately via EEG.

When the Buddhist monks were meditating, the amplitude of these gamma waves increased by 600 to 700 times. They were evenly distributed through the whole brain and synchronised. This points to a completely different state of consciousness, even if it is not clear to us precisely what it would be like to experience this state of consciousness.

We do know, though, by asking the monks, that fear is not present!

What would a world without fear be like? What would change within this context? The World is as it is because we thought it, imagined it this way. Simple as that. We are all responsible for the World as we find it. Nothing outside of the natural World need be as it is. *"You are the world; the world is you."*

When we are only experiencing the World and ourselves through thinking, we always imagine the future or remember the past. We are never actually present to see the now. We are always living in fear and acting from it. If we continue to be lost in our own little worlds created by thinking, we will forever be limited by it, reduced to our own little fears and insecurities. We will die having never lived! The World will remain divided and fearful!

As long as we live by our images and words, there will always be hurt and pain. We cannot conform to any ideologies, concepts, religious dogmas or anything else born of ideas.

To move past these images, thoughts, and ideas, the mind must be completely still. Completely silent. Only then can we find out what it would be like to live in a world without ideas.

We cannot achieve this for ourselves. You cannot centre yourself and force your mind to be quiet. This happens when you rest and just let go. Here in this landscape of Wholeness, you come to understand the real meaning of the word Love, and you realise that death is nothing to fear.

The primary fear, the fear of death, is put to rest.

A world without ideas is a world where each person acts according to Intelligence as it manifests in them, in the moment, free from the limitations of fear and conditioning.

"The way to use life

is to do nothing

through acting,

The way to use life

is to do everything

through being."

Lao-Tzu

Chapter Six

Multiple Model Agnosticism

With the juxtaposition of thinking technically and psychologically, we need to find a way of making the most of our technical knowledge without it having too firm a hold over us – otherwise, it gets to the point when it starts to bring about disorder and disproportionate emotional responses.

To understand the significant role that perspective plays and how this shapes our understanding of the World around us, I will use the everyday subject of time as an example.

It goes without saying that all observations, scientific or otherwise, take place from the perspective of someone's brain somewhere. Therefore, there is always a limit to our objectivity and the scope of our vision, whatever science says.

We can design ways to look at things more objectively, but there is always a subjective nature to everything we do.

Coming back to the subject of time, we know from our personal perspective that time can either seem to go very quickly or very slowly. We have all had experiences where we are fully absorbed in doing something, look up at the clock and realise, to our surprise, that hours have gone by.

Equally, we have all been stuck somewhere with our heads full of future fun that is waiting for us just as soon as we can leave. Those hours can go by painfully slowly.

We know that, in both instances, the hands have moved around the clock at the same speed, but due to the role perspective plays, it just doesn't feel like it. The reason we have days of 24 hours and our clocks are ordered as they are links to a full rotation of the Earth relative to the Sun, which takes on average 24 hours and 235 seconds. We can all appreciate this from our individual perspectives; we see the Sun come up and go down as the Earth rotates. This brings us to a brilliant quirk of perspective. As we sit and watch the Sun go down, we are actually rotating backwards away from the Sun.

Relative to us, the Sun is staying exactly where it is. How often, if we are honest to ourselves, does this occur to us? A calendar year is linked to a complete revolution of the Earth around the sun, taking 365 and ¼ days (which is why we have a leap year every four years).

A week being seven days is loosely relatable to the cycle of the moon.

All this makes sense as it is very convenient to organise a time to start work, fix a time to meet a friend, etc. It allows us to say that I will meet you as the Sun reaches its highest point at 12pm for lunch. Things become a little more difficult if you want to have a phone call with someone on the other side of the World. The time for me here in England, as I write this, is 14.57pm on a Saturday afternoon. In Australia, it is 23.57pm on the same day, the 10th of April, 2021. These different times means that our perspectives of the now are different if you are in Australia or in the U.K. For me, I am starting to think about what I want to cook for dinner. For my friends in Australia, they will probably have eaten and either moved on to other entertainments or will be asleep. The same now experienced differently, from a different perspective.

Another quirk of perspective is if I was on a video call to a friend in Australia. I generally would assume that what was on the screen was exactly what my friend was doing right now. The only problem with this is that it isn't. There is the time it takes for the image to reach me from Australia, a few milliseconds. The time it takes for my eyes and brain to translate the image, a few nanoseconds. If we were based much further away in space, the time it would take for the image or the voice to reach me would increase significantly. This means that the relationship to time and the idea of now is relative to the person and to where we are situated in the Universe. There is no definitive now. Time is relative, and our understanding of it is bound up in perspective.

When considering time, we must look at Albert Einstein's 'General theory of relativity'. He taught us that any large mass affects time and space around it.

If we took two friends, one of whom moved to live on the top of a mountain and the other to live at the bottom, the friend at the top of the mountain will age faster than the friend living at the bottom. There is even a fractional difference between the time experienced by your feet and your head. If you are standing up, your feet are ageing more slowly. Unfortunate as no one really looks at your feet, it is fractional, but it's still happening.

This is further complicated by another of Einstein's observations – that speed slows time down.

Again, if we took the example of the same two friends, one spent a lot of time sitting doing nothing, and the other friend was constantly on the go, the friend on the move would experience less time than the friend sitting down.

If they both carried a plant, the plant with the friend just sitting down would have more time to grow. Different experiences linked to different perspectives.

Let's look closely at the idea that time is continuously flowing along like a river as it appears to us, from our perspective. This, too, is not strictly accurate. Quantum physics, as we have said, is the attempt to understand what the World is like at a sub-atomic quantum level. How would we experience the World if we could shrink ourselves down to this microscopic landscape?

Regarding time, this is called quantum gravity. At this microscopic level, we see that time is, in fact, granular. It is better viewed as hopping along from one fragment of time to another, not linear as we might experience it. This minute fragment of time, which is as small as you can divide time up into, is called Planck time and is a hundred millionth of a trillionth of a trillionth of a trillionth of a second. You can be sure that a few of those went by as you read that!

From our perspective, we would struggle to notice a tenth of a second, let alone Planck time, but it still exists at the quantum level. The reason we don't notice it is down to perspective.

Equally, if we were not based on Earth, the idea of a 24-hour day or a year being 365 and ¼ days would also have no relevance. It is only relevant to us as it is helpful for us from our perspective in our day to day lives here on Earth. This way of looking at time has no relevance beyond this.

All the above models around time are valid at different times and in different situations. No one model has more validity or is truer than another.

Multiple model agnosticism is an idea put forward by Robert Anton Wilson. It asserts that all models are a reductionistic viewpoint of a simple or complex movement or event within a wholeness. Different models, depending on their accuracy or application, will be helpful at different times in different situations. If we are arranging when to meet up, we definitely don't need to concern ourselves with Planck time. When we hang on to the idea that these models are absolute truth, disagreement, confusion, and disorder occur.

This viewpoint sits very well with Krishnamurti's and Leary's ideas about thinking and the images, words, and ideas that are brought to bear by them – how we should be agnostic to all models of thought if we really want to be free and experience life to its fullest.

The problem is that models and images bought forward from thinking and perspective are very convincing and part of the constant conditioning applied to us by our understanding of the World around us. As we have said, seeing ourselves rotating backwards away from the Sun instead of the Sun going down is not easy or intuitive. This point that we experience things from a particular perspective makes it very hard to see that these models of thought are not truth.

For me, religious ideology and dogma sit in the realm of thinking too. Therefore, they are no more than models or concepts.

Robert Anton Wilson is saying we should, by all means, use all these models as the moment requires. The best model is the one relative to the situation, but don't hold on too tight. IT IS NOT TRUTH.

Don't use these models to define your life and the life of others. Don't beat others over the head with them to make yourself feel superior or clever. The quote below is Robert Anton Wilson's beautiful summary of this topic:

"All statements are true in some sense. False in some sense. Meaningless in some sense. True and false in some sense. True and meaningless in some sense. False and meaningless in some sense. And true and false and meaningless in some sense."

All models have limits. Einstein's models, their corresponding equations and quantum models, are critically important but not compatible with each other.

There is no overriding model yet discovered to bring everything together, and it is unlikely to come along. If we use 'Multiple Model Agnosticism', we don't have to become emotionally invested in any particular model or concept. We are free to use the model or concept that we feel is most useful practically or artistically in the moment. We can then continue to evolve technically without backing ourselves into non-sensical corners.

Chapter Seven

Order occurs outside, not inside thinking.

When we view a person purely from the perspective of the actions that derive from their thinking, we narrow our viewpoint to a tiny fragment, a little dot.

To start from this perspective when in relationship is a commonplace travesty. To view any living thing in this way robs you of so much beauty. It robs you of the ability really to see the essence of that person. It also reinforces our belief that the mind is king. We end up viewing nature and the Universe as ultimately deficient, therefore dependent for survival on our own 'brilliant minds'! This is ignorance on a grand scale, as we have already established.

If we can move away from the idea that real intelligence, with a capital I, is derived from thought, we might at last glimpse the Whole.

Outside of time, language, image, and myth. We might at last get to see beauty and to understand what real Love is; to see that Intelligence is everywhere in the natural order around us; to understand that everything intimate with the Whole movement acts from Intelligence, that none of it derives from thought.

To understand this reality in ourselves is to be in touch with your true self, genuinely to know yourself, to know what it feels like to be completely free.

In this landscape of Wholeness, we instinctively know that order arises from outside of thinking and that trying to control yourself and everything else through willpower and the application of knowledge is the very definition of futility. To quote my teacher

Jim Jealous D.O *"You have a plan. That's great, but it isn't going to work. We are more powerless, not weaker than we believe."*

When we think about how many things in the World we are not aware of at any given time, our level of arrogance is revealed. We believe we can dominate the Universe, to make it move and perform like a dancing monkey to suit our own ends.

To highlight how little we are aware of at any given moment, I will start with the simple, very British task of making a cup of tea.

Let us begin with the inclination to have a drink. Is this your thirst reflex leading you to seek a drink, or the need for caffeine, or habit, or boredom, or a combination of these?

Many things are happening automatically in your body all of the time of which we are entirely unaware. Science has allowed us to understand a good many of these things, but not in real-time. It is important to point out that the body was happily carrying out all these functions before we thought to start looking at the details.

We have a thirst reflex that will instinctively tell us we need a drink, if we use it. We often override this reflex as we are constantly not listening to our body. We are just too busy, which means we lose contact with it. It stops talking to us.

This is also true when we are hungry. If we are attuned to our instincts, they will let us know what type of foods we need to consume, in what quantity, and when. Instinct will tell us when we need the loo and if we need to be wary in any given situation.

What and when we eat and drink can be the product of instinct or, more often than not, thought. Instinct occurs outside of thinking and is part of natural law. Whether from thought or instinct, in this moment, we want a drink and have opted for a cup of tea. Why tea? That's another question!

Think about all the other things that are going on at this moment. What nerves are firing to move which muscles as you lift the kettle and fill it with water to boil?

What is happening at a molecular and sub-atomic level as you pour the boiling water into the cup and it meets the teabag?

What effect is this having on the molecules and atoms that make up the cup and the air around it?

What is happening in the ground, you stand on, in the street, you live on, the flora in the garden, the atmosphere, the Earth, the solar system, the Universe?

Seen in this way, the Universe has its own order, a series of events at a level of dizzying magnitude, all in constant movement that is neither mechanistic nor predictable. Can you really hope through your incomplete thinking to master all of this? Can anyone? Why then do we continue to operate as if we can?

If we want to change radically, internally, psychologically, as put forward by Krishnamurti, the reality that order is not a product of thought has to be with us always.

Think of it not as an idea, but a living, breathing reality inside us, where we are at peace within this movement and recognise the innate Intelligence, love it for everything it has done and continues to do for us. Trust in it.

In this landscape, we find we need no leaders, authority, dogma, or religion. We just need to feel our own essence and unique movement; to feel Intelligence as it manifests through us. We are not trying to be enlightened; we are only trying to be ourselves!

We are constantly unfolding in this movement. There is no endpoint at which we reach perfection.

To quote Rumi, *"you are not a drop in the ocean, you are a drop that contains an ocean."*

I am what is called a bio-dynamic osteopath. Via this fantastic job, I have begun to form a relationship with Intelligence and begin to see what it means for us in terms of our Health and the environment.

In the profession, we say that Intelligence (Or, as we say, the ocean) knows us. We know it's there, but our understanding of it is limited. One of the things that has interested me greatly in recent years is learning about rewilding projects. These projects show in beautiful clarity the point I am making. I am going to use the Knepp estate in England as a perfect example. Please look at the videos on their website to see for yourself the landscapes that have emerged there.

The Knepp estate extends over 3,500 acres on the south coast of England. It has been owned by the Burrell family for generations. After taking the estate over from his grandparents in 1983, Charlie Burrell attempted to run the farm in a modern way: intensive farming, using fertilisers and pesticides to grow crops. He was also rearing cows for dairy.

The land at the estate makes this kind of farming difficult as it is set on 320 meters of heavy low weald clay upon a bedrock of limestone. People were known to disappear into the clay in the past when it was wet. Stories were told of people lifting a hat up off the ground only to find it was still attached to a head!

As other farms in better locations became more and more efficient, it became apparent to the family that they were not going to be able to keep up, which put them in a very precarious position financially.

In 2000 they made the decision to sell the dairy herd and all the farm machinery to clear their debts and try a new kind of conservation put forward by Dutch ecologist Dr Frans Vera.

Dr Vera put forward the idea that after the last ice age the land in Europe would have been shaped by the grazing animals present at this time, such as European bison, elk, wild horses, wild ox, European beaver, wild boar, red deer and roe deer, bears, lynx, wolves, and wolverine. He argues that they would have been about in vast numbers similar to those seen in Africa today.

He maintained that the land was shaped by different grazing techniques and methods of physical disturbance (trampling, puddling, rootling, rubbing, snapping branches and de-barking trees), together with their ability to transfer nutrients and disperse seeds over broad areas.

It was often previously assumed that the U.K would have been completely covered in forest. In contrast, Frans Vera's ideas asserted that the grazing animals would have shaped the land. In areas where a lot of grazing took place, you would have glades of grazing lawns. You would also have scrub, groves, forests, and thorny thickets. He maintained that this landscape would constantly be shifting and changing. It was, in essence, a balance between animals and vegetation. It would have been complex and full of biodiversity.

Dr Vera asserted, *"the intention is not to recreate the past. That will always be impossible. Our World is irrevocably changed. But we can try and create something interesting and valuable with nature, using the components that are left to us."*

It was with this concept that in 2002 the Burrells ring-fenced the estate, removed any hedgerows and ditches and slowly added the nearest related animals to the original grazers. They introduced longhorn cows, red and roe deer, wild horses and Tamworth pigs. It is not at the moment legal in the U.K to re-introduce wild boar, beavers, bears, lynx, wolves or wolverines.

Initially, the first thing to happen was that the insect population started to re-build. The smaller birds then returned, then the birds of prey. The grazing animals were left to feed themselves, to look after themselves. They are not fed in any other way.

Due to the lack of apex predators and U.K law, a sensible amount of animals are culled each year, and any naturally dying animal must be moved; otherwise, everything is left to its own devices.

The soil has changed entirely since 2002 and is now shown to hold onto thousands of tons of carbon, as well as completely changing regarding bacteria, humous, worms, etc. Unlike trees that will die or be burnt, the soil will continue to hold onto the carbon it has absorbed.

Since its beginning, turtle doves, butterflies like the purple emperor, all British owl species, peregrine falcons, and storks have returned and have bred again. The vegetation has completely shifted, as Dr Vera suggested.

All this positive change has happened because they have left nature alone and have allowed the natural order of things to re-emerge.

They have understood that order happens outside of thinking!

This project has shown how quickly nature returns to balance when we stop trying to control things and accept that our application of knowledge is not a match for the natural Intelligence inherent within Wholeness.

It shows us how we need to give nature back in as many areas as is possible, on land and in the sea, if we want a positive future – to understand that we are nature, that nature is us. We are not the king of the castle but part of the Whole.

My profession is learning how this order manifests within us, how we might employ these laws of healing to improve our own health, in the same way, both psychologically and physically.

In the end, Wholeness not only means that everything is one, that everything is part of the same interconnected Whole. It also means that everything within this is always seeking to express order and Health via an Intelligence that is arising outside of our thinking.

Chapter Eight

Meditation

I want to approach the subject of meditation first from the perspective of Krishnamurti – the quote I gave at the start of this book is from his sixth talk, in 1978, which took place in Madras. It is a talk on this very subject.

The talk is titled *"Can the brain renew itself?"*

The question we are asking in this book is can we change radically, psychologically?

What, if anything, does meditation have to do with this question? What is meditation?

What are we hoping to achieve when we meditate? How much of what is taught as meditation or mindfulness sits in the landscape of thought?

I am going to start here with why we might need the brain to renew itself. As we have found out culturally, we live in a world utterly obsessed with thought. Within this movement or landscape of thinking, we have become excessively focused on ourselves. We see ourselves as separate from everything and existing within our self-defined parameters. We are forever thinking about how we are doing in relation to everyone and everything else, constantly worrying about how others perceive us.

We worry about our status in society, what power we have, how wealthy we are, how successful we are. We concern ourselves with our state of mind 'I am anxious, I am depressed, I am not happy enough'. Our internal psychology is a constant preoccupation. We concern ourselves with our relationships, our sex lives, what we own, what we don't own, how we look, how we don't look. So, it goes on, on, and on.

We worry about the same things in relation to those close to us. We form endless plans for those people close to us. We are spending virtually our entire lives fully engrossed only in this kind of thinking! A good question to ask at this point is, what are you missing while all this is going on? I mean, it is boring even writing about it!

All this constant thought, and any unresolved trauma within us, creates pressure. A lot of pressure. This pressure builds as it is ongoing and becomes greater, and greater, and greater.

Pressure, as we know, creates distortion and eventually will cause damage. This distortion and damage we know all too well in the form of emotional pain, Illness, physical pain, physical tension and restriction, migraines, neurotic behaviour, anxiety, depression, high blood pressure, reflux, irritable bowel disease, reduced immune system function, the list goes on. So, can the brain and the body renew themselves? Do we need external drugs or medical procedures to bring this renewal about?

We have covered in a previous chapter how we can think technically without becoming attached emotionally to the ideas and concepts that sit in this landscape, to rationally apply the best model possible to the situation in front of us at that moment. To apply knowledge in this way would be considered a mechanistic approach. What we cannot do in the landscape of meditation is to be mechanical.

To continue to approach meditation in the landscape of thinking in the long term is, put simply, a waste of time. It would be like practising a recipe that you love using the wrong ingredients. You could practice forever, and it would still not taste right. So here lies the difficulty.

Most people new to meditation are by definition living almost exclusively in the landscape of thought. They have spent many years navigating and processing the World through the mind only. Therefore, when they inquire into meditation, they do so from this landscape and from this perspective. They want to know precisely what they need to do – to have a mechanical model to follow – how to sit, what they should be chanting or doing. They are trying to understand meditation from the perspective of thinking.

During their initial attempts at meditation, the mind will forever be intruding, trying to apply thinking to what is happening; trying to employ previous experience and ways of seeing the World in order to make sense of mediation. This is, as we will see, a juxtaposition. It is also true that we all have to start somewhere.

Meditation involves the art of listening, of seeing, and of learning. For example, I cannot expect to learn anything new if I am forever viewing everything through the lens of my previous ideas, words, and images. I cannot really be in a relationship with anything if something else sits between me and my thinking, words, or imagery.

All the words, images and concepts from the past prevent me from really seeing the subject in the now. Equally, if as I am listening to someone I am forever analysing, agreeing or disagreeing, I am not really listening with any freedom. Therefore, nothing new can occur. I cannot learn.

So, part of mediation would be a mind in a quiet enough state to actually see something like a tree, plant, or person and to have no words, analysis, or imagery between it and you.

Have a quick go now. What happens?

Even when we do manage to really see someone or something, notice how quickly the mind kicks in:

'What's happening?

'How do we label that?'

'How will I explain this experience to others?'

Don't try to change this or stop it; just notice it. It always makes me smile. It's amusing.

The mind, the ego, is incapable of the art of seeing, listening, and learning.

Hopefully, we can move away then from the more mechanistic forms of mediation where we are sitting in a specific posture for such and such a time with one part of the mind observing, another wishing it would be quiet or different.

In this scenario, one part of the mind, which we can call the observer, is looking at another part of the mind, which we will call the observed. This has created an artificial division in the mind, which is called a duality. It sets up a scenario when one part of your mind tries to control another part of your mind, naturally creating internal conflict.

Hope you are keeping up with this!

As we have learned previously, our consciousness is its contents; we have explored this idea. We know then that both the part of the mind acting as the observer and the part being observed are part of the same content.

The observing part of the mind is not a higher mind, a better mind. It is just a different corner of the same mind.

I hope we can see that this is not helpful and creates more internal conflict and disorder! I must point out that the Buddhist intention behind mindfulness is that you just notice what is, without analysis. Still, the above example is what most people end up doing.

The other common type of mediation is repeating mantras, which could be considered a form of self-hypnosis. If I am busying my mind with the repetition of mantras, it will have the action of preventing thinking. I am not saying this is a bad thing, but it isn't the complete quiet and freedom that occurs in meditation. It might well take us there!

Meditation then is a completely free mind, a mind with limitless space, completely free of fear. A mind that sees Wholeness sees that order happens outside of thought – a mind that can sit inside a question without seeking any answers – A mind vibrating with gamma brain waves.

To give you an idea of what not seeking answers means, it is called 'sitting in the question'. I would like to invite you to close your eyes after reading this paragraph. I would like you to imagine a vast empty space full of everything you don't know. Imagine being in this space now. Everything you don't know amounts to a lot, whoever you are!

What does it feel like to be in this vast space?

To me, it is a huge relief. There is no pressure to know, or to be, anything. I feel supported and held in this space.

What is holding me? Meditation allows us to be taken to a silent landscape, a vast space full of Wholeness, full of Love.

This is the movement of meditation. We are whole, adaptable, and un-mechanistic. Here our mind and body can renew themselves. Here we can change radically, internally, psychologically.

Osteopathy, I believe, has a lot to offer on how we might arrive at a perfectly tranquil mind without applying any force or will.

It is true that you cannot centre yourself. You cannot, through willpower, bring about a meditative state in yourself. This will happen only if you rest and let go. Then something will centre you.

We are resting, sitting in a meeting place, and here we can be centred.

Krishnamurti: *"Anyone who knows this place is blessed."*

Chapter Nine

What has Osteopathy got to do with anything?

Andrew Taylor Still:

"To find health should be the object of the doctor. Anyone can find disease."

Until now, we have spoken about ideas and people that have been in the public arena for many years. The next stage of our journey together links to my work as a biodynamic osteopath.

For most, it will be a new way to view normal and the idea of health in general.

A good question that is surprisingly not often asked in the medical World will be, what is our starting point here:

What is normal?

It sounds obvious, but where are we trying to get to if we do not understand what normal is? How do we know if something is wrong? My field of osteopathy is based right here, in this question.

I must explain now that osteopathy has a few different branches. Within the profession, there are many ways of thinking and working. This will largely depend on the individual's way of viewing themselves, their patients, and the World around them.

It is not my intention to suggest that my viewpoint is the only way of working, or that other ways of treating have no value. A person can only work within their own experience.

It is true, though, that many osteopaths working around the World might not recognise what I am describing here, and indeed may be affronted by it.

In the UK where I work, what we are about to talk about is not a way of working that is celebrated or considered particularly desirable by my governing body.

Obviously I think this is a shame. I mention it because I know many of you reading this will not recognise the type of osteopathy I put forward here. Instead, you will have an image of someone that mobilises joints (clicks them), articulates, and works on muscles with direct action. Those based in America might think of osteopaths as akin to an allopathic Doctor.

In the UK, Osteopathy is still described officially as being holistic; but in the profession, evidence-based practice is actually at the steering wheel. We don't have to look too hard to see that Wholeness, and looking at a fraction of the whole (which evidence-based practice is) is a juxtaposition. The two, are in essence, fundamentally different.

The initial degree I took in Osteopathy was grounded in science with a very allopathic slant. As an Osteopath, I was taught anatomy to a very detailed level: neurology, pathology, physiology, embryology (Vitally important to an osteopath), nutrition, exercise, osteopathic structural technique, and some osteopathic philosophy. This was a great foundation and was very well taught. It did, though, struggle to offer any coherent view of Wholeness and holistic practice.

Holistic practice has to be based on 'wholeness' by definition, wholeness being that everything is one and everything is a part of an interconnected whole.

I used to think, as a student, that my colleagues were somehow able to process all of what was happening in their patients purely through the application of knowledge. I used to think it was just me that was not up to this task.

We know now after the previous chapters that thinking is fragmented and limited and cannot see Wholeness.

I now know that, in essence, the idea of holistic practice was not in my training. It was primarily lip service and had nothing to do with the idea of everything being part of an interconnected whole with implicit order.

It was a well-taught degree offering a good grasp of what we can understand via knowledge. I continue to study all of these areas and many more as they develop and advance. Working holistically is never an excuse not to study properly. It is true, though, that if we put together every book ever written about human beings, it would still be an incomplete picture.

The words and the images are not the thing.

For many years I worked as an Osteopath within the context of my initial training. I used massage, articulation, mobilisation, education and advice to try and help my patients. I was though unhappy in myself and had an instinctually uncomfortable feeling about using many of these techniques. I was stuck in the landscape of thinking and did not knowingly step out of it at this point.

I was not what you would have called very balanced at this time.

After a few years, I started to do courses in craniosacral osteopathy, of which biodynamics is a branch. The courses, to me, were fantastic and revelatory. They were based on the ideas of William Sutherland, an osteopath who we will meet later. This, at last, was a window into what I feel is real osteopathy.

Then a colleague mentioned the name Jim Jealous to me in conversation, and it was like a little bell went off in my head. This little bell is an excellent example of a 'still small voice'. I went home that day and found a beginner's lecture given by Jim and listened in a slightly bemused way to what he said.

It is apparent now in retrospect that I had not understood much of what he said. Luckily, as has been the way of things for me in this area, the correct series of events were waiting for me anyway.

The day after I listened to Jim's lecture, a friend of mine called concerning a chronic pain he had been having in the abdomen. It had been present for many years and had been investigated many times by consultants and via various scans etc., and deemed nothing sinister. No diagnosis had ever been put forward. I mentioned this new way of working I would like to try, and he agreed to be treated.

During the treatment, what I now know to be a stillness emerged. This is a profound event, especially if it is new to you. My eyes started to shake and, like Monty pythons' dead parrot, I felt like I might fall sideways off my chair. The room was filled with subtle light. My friend was oblivious to all of it and I wasn't going to volunteer this bizarre information.

After the stillness had dissipated and a neutral manifested, my friend got up and left. He phoned me later that week to say that the pain had gone.

I have been working for years now to make sense of what happened. I believe this event was given to me.

You might find what I have just said hard to believe. I would be surprised if you just accepted it. Let us go to the beginnings of Osteopathy and work forward to see if we can make sense of it.

Osteopathy has a lot to offer us regarding answering our question, 'Can we change radically, psychologically?' It teaches us how the body and mind can renew and form better internal connections to create a cohesive whole – teaching us more about who we are and how order manifests in us personally.

The original osteopath was a man called Andrew Taylor Still, a name not well known outside the profession of Osteopathy and some might argue not well understood within the profession either.

He was a freethinking and completely independent man who was not perturbed by the cultural rules or narratives around him.

It is essential to appreciate that Still achieved what he achieved because he did not buy into the idea that we should automatically respect the authority of the common narrative – doctors, scientists, ministers, and politicians – but we should find out for ourselves.

"The explorer of truth must first declare his independence" is a quote from Still that echoes what we have heard from Krishnamurti's ideas: *"He must establish his observatory on hills of his own; he must establish it above the imaginary high planes of rulers, kings, professors of schools of all kinds and denominations. He must be the Czar of his own mental empire."* This quote shows how firmly Still held on to this fundamental idea of freedom of thought.

Like Krishnamurti and Leary, Still had an unusual and interesting life. Still's father Abram, one of 15 children, was born in North

Carolina in 1796. Abram's father Boaz was a slaveholding, heavy drinking gambler by all accounts. As a child, Abram was introduced to methodism by one of Boaz's slave workers and became a very devout Methodist, eventually becoming a travelling minister.

In 1822 Abram married Andrew's mother, Martha Moore, who came from a farming family and settled down in Jonesville, Virginia. There, the family bought a cabin and 500 acres. Abram also studied medicine and qualified as an MD to supplement his ministerial salary.

Andrew Taylor Still was born on the 6th of August 1828. Like Krishnamurti, Andrew's early experiences of school were not favourable. With Still describing his first school as a *"place of torture"*. Andrew was poor at spelling and was regularly beaten with a cane there. He was saved from this misery in 1834 when Abram excepted a new ministerial posting in Macon County, Missouri. Here were the beginnings of the national argument that would end in the American Civil War. Abram felt strongly that holding slaves was a sin (which was not a popular view in Virginia at that time). This, in the end, is what facilitated this move and others in the future.

The family sold their land and animals and, with $900, set off across the country in two wagons. Along the way, a fellow minister prayed on Abram's trust in religious people convincing him to lend him $700 as a loan that he would repay with interest. The money was never returned. This turn of events forced the family to live life right on the edge in a wild and remote part of the country.

The family used their remaining money to purchase land in Barnesville, Missouri, a mixture of woodland and prairie with a natural spring. They also bought livestock in the form of two cows. While here in 1938, Mary had her seventh child. The family worked to establish a farm, with every member of the family working hard. They planted crops and hunted what they could, things like deer, turkey, duck, quail, and squirrel. The meat was preserved via smoking, and the skins turned into shoes, jackets, and short trousers.

As the farm grew, the family started to grind their own flour and saw their own wood. They introduced horses, mules, cattle, pigs, and sheep – a lot of work for the children and Martha, as Abram was often away in his role as a minister.

In the 5 years the family were in Missouri, they only went to school for one short 3-month stint. In the summer, they were expected to work on the farm. In the winter, they were home-schooled in Methodist literature and from Abram's medial texts, which were the books they had.

Abram was very strict when it came to his religion and Andrew was expected to learn whole passages of scripture under threat of violence. Apparently he did not relate well to this overbearing religious ideology.

Andrew was always interested in anatomy. As he had to hunt, smoke, and store the meat, he would essentially dissect the animals to understand more about their anatomy and how they functioned. This was accompanied by reading Abram's anatomy books.

Of his upbringing, Still felt it had been superior to a *"civilised"* upbringing – full of clean air, a plain natural diet, and lots of outdoor exercise, which he believed to be essential to good physical and mental development. It also meant he thought less through words, as most people do, and more, as one of his later students reported, in terms of *"pictures, events, forces, and wholes."*

For most of us, our connection to nature is increasingly frayed and often further obscured by our education. To grow up in such undisturbed nature, as Still did, is hard for us to imagine today. To survive in the natural World, according to family needs, was to understand it not in theory, but as a living reality. This allowed for a sense of being part of a natural movement to develop, which allowed Andrew to see Wholeness as a living reality without education and conditioning getting in the way.

In 1849, age 20, Andrew married Mary Vaughn, and their first daughter Marusha was born in December the following year. At this time, Andrew became a teacher in a small school. The couple then had a son, Abraham, in November 1852. Just before that, Andrew's father called him to help practice medicine in a Shawnee reserve.

Abram had started working as an MD at the reservation a year before. He had quickly become overwhelmed with the size of the job. Native American tribes had been forcibly moved and continuously tricked out of their land by the advancing Europeans and had ended up in various reserves around America, which stood for the complete collapse of their previous lives. It goes without saying that this was an ugly process full of lies and violence of every description. They had had no chance.

Andrew became popular on the reservation, learning the Shawnee language and, in doing so, a lot of their history, traditions, stories and beliefs.

Far from being non-religious, as was commonly assumed by western culture, Andrew came to understand that the Shawnee believed in the 'Great Spirit or Creator' that was the source of and a part of everything.

"They believed in self-control and complete honesty. Each person was his or her own judge, responsible not only for their own behaviour but for the behaviour of all. Elders were very respected. Children were taught that the Great Creator loves all equally and therefore to injure, wrong, or hate another was to injure oneself. To do good to another person and make them happy was to make yourself happy. They had no concept of ownership, of rich and poor. If you had more than you needed you gave it to those that needed it."

The following passage is taken from the book 'Neither Wolf nor Dog' by Kent Nerburn. It looks at one of the significant differences between Western and Native American cultures. The passage shows that there were cultures that lived with freedom and honour at its heart. It was also a culture that prized silence above everything. Many of the ideas in this book are also echoed in "Neither Wolf nor Dog". This particular passage is about the difference between freedom and honour and takes place between Kent Nerburn and an Indian Elder called Dan:

"...I think it's because the most important thing for white people is freedom. The most important thing for Indian people is honour.

This is why white people have listened to the black people more than to us Indians. The black people want freedom, too, just like white people. And since the white people took freedom from the black people, the whites feel guilty about the blacks. You see what I am saying?

But the Indian has always been free. We are free today. We have always been freer than the white man, even when he first came here. When you came to our shore your people wore clothes made out of chains. Our people wore nothing at all. Yet you tried to bring us freedom.

The white World puts all the power at the top, Nerburn. When someone gets to the top, they have the power to take your freedom. When your people first came to our land they were trying to get away from those people at the top. But they still thought the same, and soon there were new people at the top in the new country. It's just the way you were taught to think.

In your churches there is someone at the top.

In your schools too. In your government. In your business. There is always someone at the top and that person has the right to say whether you are good or bad. They own you.

No wonder Americans always worry about freedom.

You have so damn little of it. If you don't protect it, someone will take it away from you. You have to guard it every second, like a dog guards a bone.

When you came among us, you couldn't understand our way. You wanted to find the person at the top. You wanted to find the fences that bound us – how far our land went, how far our government went. Your World was made of cages and you thought ours was, too. Even though you hated your cages you believe in them. They defined your World and you needed them to define ours.

Our old people notice this from the beginning.

They said that the white man lived in a world of cages, and that if we didn't look out, they would make us live in a world of cages too.

So we started noticing. Everything looked like cages. Your clothes fit like cages. Your houses looked like cages. You put fences around your yards so they looked like cages. Everything was a cage. You turned the land into cages. Little squares.

Then after you had all the cages you made a government to protect these cages. And that government was all cages. All laws about what you couldn't do. The only freedom you had was inside your own cage. Then you wondered why you weren't happy and didn't feel free. You made all the cages, then you wondered why you didn't feel free.

We Indians never thought that way. Everyone was free. We didn't make cages of law or land. We believed in honour. To us the white man looked like a blind man walking. He knew he was on the wrong path when he bumped into the edge of one of the cages. Our guide was inside, not outside. It was honour . It was more important for us to know what was right than to know what was wrong.

We looked at the animals and saw what was right.

We saw how the deer would trick the more powerful animals and how the bear would make her children strong by running them without mercy.

We saw how the buffalo would stand and watch until it understood. We saw how every animal had wisdom and we tried to learn that wisdom. We would look to them to see how they got along and how they raised their young. Then we would copy them. We did not look for what was wrong. Instead we always reached for what was right.

It was this search that kept us on a good path, not rules and fences. We wanted honour for ourselves and our families. We wanted others to say, 'He is a good man. He is as brave as the bear' or 'as clean as the fox.'

We had freedom so we didn't seek it. We sought honour, and honour was duty, so he was weak.

The only time freedom is important is when others are trying to put you in chains. We had no chains so we needed no freedom."

To Andrew, these ideas around freedom, spirituality, and Wholeness resonated a divine intelligence that created and breathed the World and everything in it, that matter and spirit were part of the same interwoven whole, that nature and the creator were one. Therefore, in nature there was inherently a sacred wisdom. The central tenet of these ideas was that the Earth and water should not be harmed – the opposite of western ideology, religious or otherwise.

To the Native Americans, the Earth does not belong to Man to be plundered and pillaged; Man belongs to the Earth. This upbringing, fully immersed in and dependent upon nature, was similar to Andrews in many ways. After a year of working medically in a western way at the reserve, Andrew returned to Macon county.

At this time, the disagreement over slavery was building to a national crescendo.

In 1854 Drew officially *"chose the side of freedom"*, and the family left for Kansas. Here Andrews medical practice continued amidst increasing violence and instability. As the troubles increased, both Andrew and Abram became marked men by proslavery groups. They had to live with a group of families moving from house to house with the men sleeping in the surrounding bush armed with their guns.

Andrew continued to practice medicine, tackling increasingly difficult war injuries. He worried that his anatomical knowledge was not good enough to treat these injuries. It is easy with stab wounds and bullet wounds to damage an artery or a nerve. It was essential to understand what had been damaged and how he would go about treating these wounds without causing further harm.

In response to this concern, Andrew went to a Shawnee and Delaware burial ground. He went both under cover of darkness and in the daytime, where there were shallow graves. Here he dissected and preserved bodies and removed bones for further study. He later said:

"The dead Indians never objected to being object-lessons for the development of science. Their relatives knew nothing about it; and as 'where ignorance is bliss it is folly to be wise,' and as the knowledge which I gained by this research has aided me to relieve countless thousands of suffering human beings, and snatch many from the grave, I shall not allow my equanimity of mind to be disturbed by the thoughts that I once sought knowledge from Indian bones."

In 1859 Stills wife Mary died. History does not reveal to us the cause of her death. Andrew was left at 31, a single father of three children, his third child, Susan having been born three years earlier.

Three months later, Andrew meets and marries a physician's daughter, Mary Elvira Turner. The couple would go on to become parents to a daughter called Marcia.

In 1864 an unimaginable tragedy occurred within the family. Meningitis was spreading through America, and all of the children except 14-year-old Marusha contracted it. Andrew called in Abram and his brother James, also and MD, to help him. All of their medical care was to no avail, and all of the children were to die. This shocking moment was to be a catalyst for Andrew:

"It was when I stood gazing upon three members of my family, all dead from disease, spinal meningitis, that I propounded to myself the serious questions: 'In sickness has God left man in a world of guessing? Guess what is the matter? What to give, and guess the result? And when dead, guess where he goes?' I decided then that God was not a guessing God but a God of truth. And all his works, spiritual and material, are harmonious. His law of animal life is absolute. So wise a God had certainly placed the remedy within the material house in which the spirit of life dwells."

Here we see the beginnings of Osteopathy being seen by Still: If there is perfect natural order in the body, soul, and spirit, then there is health. Below is the preface of Still's first book, the 'Philosophy of Osteopathy', published much later in 1899:

"Many of my friends have been anxious ever since Osteopathy became an established fact, that I should write a treatise on the science. But I was never convinced that the time was ripe for such a production, nor am I even now convinced that this is not a little premature. Osteopathy is only in its infancy, it is a great unknown

sea just discovered, and as yet we are only acquainted with its shore-tide.

When I saw others who had not more than skimmed the surface of the science, taking up the pen to write books on Osteopathy, and after having carefully examined their productions, found they were drinking from the fountains of old schools of drugs, dragging back the science to the very systems from which I divorced myself so many years ago, and realised the hungry students were ready to swallow such mental poison, dangerous as it was, I became fully awakened to the necessity of some sort of Osteopathic literature for those wishing to be informed.

This book is free from quotations from medical authors and differs from them in opinion on almost every important question. I do not expect it to meet their approval; such a thing would be unnatural and impossible.

It is my object in this work to teach principles as I understand them, and not rules. I do not instruct the student to punch or pull a certain bone, nerve or muscle for a certain disease, but by knowledge of normal and abnormal, I hope to give a specific knowledge for all diseases.

This work has been written a little at a time for several years, just as I could snatch a moment from other cares to devote to it. I have carefully compiled these thoughts into a treatise. Every principle herein laid down has been fairly well tested by myself, and proven true.

The book has been written by myself in my own way, without any ambition to fine writing, but to give to the World a start in a philosophy that may be a guide in the future.

Owing to the great haste with which the book has been rushed through the press to meet the urgent demand, we will ask the indulgence of the public for any imperfections that may appear.

Hoping the World may profit by these thoughts, I am, respectfully,

A.T. Still"

We learn from the book that Still sees the body as a single whole which he describes as a 'triune' when in balance: Body, soul, and spirit as an undivided whole.

Still believed that we can trace disease back to a cause by seeing what has changed in the structure and, therefore, the changes in function relatively. For example, embryologically, the body's midline is formed segmentally, which is the notochord structurally.

One embryological segment is half of the vertebra above and half of the vertebra below, including the neurological, vascular, and lymphatic vessels between them supplying that segment of the body.

If we see the body from a cellular perspective. We understand that every cell in the body needs to bring in what is necessary for its healthy function and excrete what is required for its healthy function. It is crucial then that there are unhindered nerves, blood vessels, and lymphatic vessels.

If we have an issue structurally or otherwise that results in any reduced function, those cells are now not operating at an optimal level. Therefore the door is now open to the possibility of disease. Something Still described as a *"withering field"*.

For Still, when the body was ordered and therefore *"normal"*, it would be healthy. It had its own *"medicine cabinet"* that could deal with whatever was thrown at it (a precursor to the knowledge of the immune system, although it had a more significant meaning than this).

It was vital for Still that an Osteopath had an intimate knowledge of anatomy in the sense of being able to visualise it perfectly.

In a western allopathic approach to medicine, we all know that the first thing to do when discovering ill health is to help the 'poor old body' with drugs, external force, or surgery.

This help is generally aimed only at symptoms. It is not a common narrative to look for the cause of disease based on the assumption that the body does not need external help if it is healthy.

As a result, we generally have little to no faith in our physical or psychological health being achieved naturally.

After the death of his three children, Still carried on practising medicine, but with these new ideas bubbling in the background. Any faith Andrew had in drugs as a treatment at that time was now gone.

The family moved once again to Baldwin City, and in 1867 Mary gave birth to twins Harry and Herman. Also, this Year Abram contracted pneumonia, and it became apparent he was not long for this World. Andrew was interested as to whether his father's constant devotion to methodism had allowed him to understand what happened after death. *"And when dead, guess where he goes?"*. Abram had nothing to offer, though. Even after spending most of his life as a Methodist preacher!

Still documented a couple of early working examples of his own ideas in action; the first was concerning himself.

On a reconnaissance run while involved in the Border War, Still was chased on horseback by a group of proslavery Missourians. In trying to escape, he took a shortcut across a 'foot log' crossing a creak. He and the mule fell, resulting in Andrew hitting his sternum (a bone at the front of your chest) on the saddle. He escaped, but the injury resulted in the onset of heart palpitations. Still suffered from these for ten years, seeking many diagnoses from doctors of: 'valvular disease of the heart'.

One day he was feeling pain in the upper back after playing croquet. He placed one of the wooden croquet balls under the thoracic spine, lay down on it and rested his legs up against a tree. He felt something move and realised that his back pain had eased and later that his palpitations had gone. They never returned.

This personal experience was followed later. Andrew was called urgently to a situation where a woman was suffering from pneumonia. The lady concerned was struggling to breathe. With no medicines available to him, Still was sitting on the bed completing an examination and thinking about what he should do.

The examination revealed pain over a specific rib which looked to be sitting incorrectly. The lady told Still that they had been hanging the carcass of a pig they had slaughtered from a tree so they could clean it. The carcass had swung free, hitting her in the chest.

Andrew examined the point at which the sore rib attached the spine and worked the joint free. Immediately the lady's pain diminished, followed an hour later by her fever breaking and her breathing returning to normal.

Andrew spent the night only to find his patient was well enough to get up in the morning.

He concluded that maybe the misplaced rib relative to the spine had altered the action of the corresponding nerves and blood vessels, resulting in venous congestion in the pleura (the outer layers of the lung). This had led to the onset of pneumonia.

He also considered the palpitations in his own case to have been caused similarly. He hypothesised that a misplaced rib head was affecting the action of the sympathetic nerves supplying the heart or its blood vessels, resulting in an irregular heartbeat.

Over time, and after treating and viewing his patients in this way, it became apparent that the spinal nerves were particularly vulnerable at the intervertebral foramen, especially when a rib's position became altered.

Still continued to treat in this way when he could, often sending his sons for placebo medicines like coloured water and balls of dough, so he didn't have to use drugs in his treatments and instead could rely on the body's natural healing forces.

At 10am on the 22nd of June 1874, Still had an epiphany. He wrote:

"Like a burst of sunshine the whole truth dawned on my mind, that I was gradually approaching a science by study, research, and observation, that would be of great benefit to the world".

This moment hinged on the idea that *"All God's work is perfect".*

This means that we move the meaning of God from a figurehead of any given religion to the idea that it stands for the divine Intelligence behind order, the perfect unfolding movement of the universe of which we are a part.

Still saw that if we are able to be 'normal,' e.g., perfectly aligned with this divine order, we are perfectly aligned with Health.

This moment of clarity occurred while in discussion with his brother James also an M.D. Later, Still would write:

"I was shot in the dome of reason by an arrow charged with the principles of philosophy. Since that day I have sacredly remembered and kept its anniversary... sometimes withdrawing from the presence of man to meditate upon the event of that day wherein I saw that the word 'God' signified perfection in all things and in all places."

He realised that every aspect of man, mind, body and spirit was permeated with divinity; that every part of man's anatomy, physiology, mind, and spirit was constantly aligned to and striving to express this divine quality known in Osteopathy as the 'Health'.

Krishnamurti's writings echo the idea that order is derived through divine intent, and disorder is established when ignored or overridden in the material world.

Krishnamurti says disorder and order are not opposites of each other. That order is not related to disorder. That order only occurs when disorder stops!

Still sees that if we only view a person from a material perspective, we create an unnecessary and illusory division of body, mind, and spirit. These images only exist in our thinking and create significant limits to our ability to help and understand ourselves and others.

This is a massive problem in the modern World, whereas Still's big problem was that his ideas were deemed heretical. They denied 'original sin' and the idea of God as a 'father in heaven'. In modern times, seeing the World in anything other than a purely material light is perceived as backward and 'not grounded in science'.

To this, Still wrote that *"Science cannot deal with fundamental questions"*.

In more detail he wrote: *"Science is only a tool or a key, and it can unlock only certain material problems.* ***It cannot appraise itself. It is not a judge but a witness****. Problems of mind, of character, moral, aesthetic, literary, artistic are not its sphere. It counts and weighs and measures and analyses, it traces relations, but it cannot appraise its own results."* It is a surprising truth that the laws of growth, healing, and repair are largely unknown to science and allopathic medicine. They are supernatural laws and natural laws – intelligent order alive in the body, mind, and spirit.

A new philosophy was necessary to see and to treat people in this light, one free from reductionism and religious dogma. Krishnamurti would not have disagreed. Still asserted now that concerning the human organism, *"you will find all that heaven and earth contain, fully represented, mind, matter and motion, blended by the wisdom of Deity."*

Going forward from this revelation, he stood firm. To Still, there was no higher authority: *"With the iron hand of will I barred the gate of memory, shut out the past with all its old ideas. My soul took on [a] receptive attitude, my ear was tuned to nature's rhythmic harmony... My spirit was o'erwhelmed with the unmeasurable magnitude of the divine plan on which the universe is constructed."*

For the Still family, this revelation marked 15 years of hardship, poverty, and ostracism by friends, family, and patients. Due to what was viewed as his heretical views, Andrew and his family moved to the town of Kirksville, in Missouri.

Over the next 10 years, the family suffered considerably so that Andrew could honour the truth of Osteopathy. He continues to think and meditate in this time and to study and to sit with nature. It takes years for the mind to become genuinely silent. He continues to build his knowledge of anatomy. Every bone is meticulously understood. Every muscular and ligamental attachment, blood vessel, nerve, viscera, and connective tissue is understood and visualised. He brings all this to bear in his treatments when they do occur.

Slowly, word of Andrew's successes, relative to allopathic medicine, begins to spread. After 20 years on the periphery of the town, and the World, this leads to an influx of patients to the town from all over America and of people wanting to study Osteopathy. This eventually led to the opening of an infirmary and The American School of Osteopathy, ASO.

By 1913, only two medical schools in America had more students and Osteopathy was legal in all but two states.

Using purely his own money, Still had built a large infirmary including a maternity ward and operating theatres (he believes surgery to be necessary as a very last resort), a school, the ASO and everything that goes with it.

He also built the first humane sanatorium, which is a beautiful building set on acres of countryside. The patients are being treated with Osteopathy, good nutritious food, and time to relax and rest. The goodwill in America was extraordinary at the time. Life magazine in 1916 wrote jokingly:

"Something unusually drastic and effective will have to be done with the osteopaths, if they continue to cure after the regular physicians have given them up. For the first offense there could be a moderate fine; if the offense is repeated, the fine could be doubled and a term of imprisonment added. The licence could also be taken away and the wicked and reprehensible osteopath would thus not be permitted to practice any more, for it is quite obvious that if osteopaths continue to cure people, the regular medical profession, which now controls the laws and liberties of the majority, might eventually go out of business."

It is extraordinary to conceive that this happened to Andrew after so many years of ostracism and ridicule. What largely seems to have happened after his death, as the years have gone by, is that the medical profession, and the reductionistic thinking therein, took over from osteopathic thinking within the profession.

This has happened to such an extent that now someone can study an osteopathic degree and never once view osteopathy!

Just so we can be completely clear here, Andrew Taylor Still was a spiritual person. He constantly built his knowledge to an extraordinary level and was very well educated in many aspects of science. When he was treating all this was forgotten:

"Once in the operating rooms (treatment rooms) *you are in a place where printed books are known no more forever. Your own native ability, with nature's book, are all that command respect*

in this field of labor. Here you lay aside the long words, and use your mind in deep and silent earnestness; drink deep from the eternal fountain of reason, penetrate the forests of that law whose beauties are life and death. To know all of a bone in its entirety would close both ends of an eternity.

Solemnity takes possession of the mind, a smile of love runs over the face, the ebbs and tides of the great ocean of reason, whose depths have never been fathomed, swell to your surging brain. You eat and drink; and as you stand in silent amazement, suns appear where you never saw a star, brilliant with the rays of God's wisdom, as displayed in man, and the laws of life, eternal in days, and as true as the mind of God Himself."

We see clearly here a meditative state of mind, as described by Krishnamurti, applied to health. We will find as we go on how this has allowed Osteopathy to build an image of man and the universe from the perspective of this landscape which will help us to "change radically, internally, psychologically".

I will leave you with a couple more quotes from Andrew Taylor Still before we move on. If you are interested in furthering your reading about him, 'A.T.STILL, From the Dry Bone to the Living Man, by John Lewis' is exemplary.

In response to the question put to him by a student, Ernest Tucker, *"Could the spirits reveal the nature of God?"* Still replied: *"God is a term by all living beings spoken mentally or vocally, signifying that I am going to lift myself above the individual and personal limitations and thoughts, and rise to the broadest freedom of thought."*

We can see clear connections with Krishnamurtis' ideas of freedom of thought, Wholeness, and Divine Intelligence.

This differs from the judgemental figurehead of many religions. ‘God’ is a word that we can find very challenging due to the connections we apply to it relative to religion and religious dogma.

Again, we need to see that the word is not the thing and not allow all these ideas and images to cloud our vision and hamper our relationship with Wholeness. Here are the last quotes I will put forward from Still:

“To your heart ever be true” and, *“It is true to the design of nature when we act our true selves.”*

If we recognise that we are part of an interconnected whole, that has a natural order. If we want to realise our part in this movement, it is essential to understand what is meant by ‘true self’ and that we learn to express it.

No more. No less.

Chapter Ten

Contributions of Thought

The next big step within Osteopathy was taken by a beautifully kind, intelligent and unassuming character, William Garner Sutherland.

Will Sutherland was born on the 27th of March 1873 to Dorinda and Robert Sutherland in the state of Wisconsin. He had two brothers, Steve and Guy, and a sister, Helen. His early childhood was characterised by constant movement. His dad Robert was a blacksmith by trade and took other jobs in farming and insurance to make ends meet. The family moved many times to places in Wisconsin, Minnesota, South Dakota, and Wyoming, generally living in smaller rural towns.

In 1885 the Sutherland family signed what was called an indenture agreement. This was a contract agreed between Will's parents and a man named George Schlosser that tied Will to an apprentice agreement, lasting an unspecified number of years. This would have given the family another wage and was a good form of education for Will.

Schlosser was in the newspaper business, which Will trained and worked in for many years, allowing him an opportunity to be around many well-educated and interesting reporters, and printers. This was a good beginning for Will; it stood him in good stead for his future profession and his life as an osteopath.

Will first became aware of osteopathy through his work as a journalist and patients' stories in the press of successful treatments. This positive viewpoint was reinforced through the successful treatment of his brother Guy, who had become very ill. Inspired by this, Will applied for a scholarship at Still's ASO in 1898 and was successful. He completed his studies at the ASO in June 1900.

Will would have seen and heard Andrew Taylor Still speak in his time at the ASO but was shy in nature and never spoke to him directly.

Will's osteopathic journey begins with a single thought: *"the thought came, like a bolt from the blue".* A disarticulated skull in a glass display case was at the ASO, brought at great cost from Paris. This was displayed in one of the main halls of the college.

Will was considering the spaces between the various cranial bones one day when he was struck by the joints between the sphenoid bone (a butterfly-shaped bone that is central to the structure of the skull) and the temporal bones (which are located on the sides of the skull and have the ear as part of their anatomy).

The joints shape and form suggested to Will that they were part of a moving mechanism linked to respiration. At the time, the common narrative was that the skull was completely fused in adults, and therefore these joints should be unmoving. Due to this overarching narrative, Will shelved the idea for a few years but kept it in mind.

Eventually the time came for Will to investigate the idea of mobility of the cranial bones.

Could he disprove the common narrative? To buy a disarticulated skull was out of his price range, so Will had to use the skull of the skeleton he had bought for his practice.

Very carefully, using a penknife, he eased apart the different cranial bones – which in itself proved that they were not fused.

Careful examination of the different types of joints found in the various bones clearly indicated movement. These first findings pushed him on.

His wife Adah writes about Will spending hours looking at and studying the various bones individually and collectively, paying particular attention to the sphenoid.

He considered the movement the individual bones were capable of and how that would work as a whole.

He understood that the bones in the cranial base were formed from cartilage and that the bones making up the vault of the skull were formed in the membranes. He knew this would allow for flexibility, and like Still was prepared to think for himself and stand on his own.

From the beginning of his work, he was looking for a 'primary respiratory mechanism', something that reflected the breath of life:

"It must be something first, with something else second...we must get back to the spark that ignites the motor...get back to the central station, and reason. Take the creation of man; the Maker breathed the Breath of Life, not the breath of air, into the nasals of a form of clay and man became a living soul...the breath of life uses the breath of air as one of the material elements in a mechanism to walk about on Earth. The human brain is a motor...it will not be found in a laboratory...."

This, in itself, is a monumental thought.

While pondering this, Will comes across an article he has read before, a piece about the 4th cranial ventricle of the brain:

"All the physiological centres including that of respiration, are located in the floor of the fourth ventricle." This becomes the spark behind the first of his many experiments carried out on himself, always accompanied by his wife, Adah. This was necessary due to the dangerous nature of what Will was doing to himself.

This humble team of two would go on to change the way we see ourselves forever. Today, nearly a hundred years later, their work has not really been fully absorbed into the day to day care we all receive.

I want to make it plain now that this book is in no way a means by which you can learn to treat someone else. The experiments I will talk about now are just examples. Working in this way takes years of experience, education, and guidance. First, do no harm. We are learning about ourselves to enable us to have a greater understanding of what we are to change radically, inwardly, and psychologically.

The first experiment Will attempted is now known as a 'CV4', a 4th ventricle compression. Will carried out all his experiments at the time via a homemade contraption comprising of, at various times, a football helmet, a precisely carved wooden bowl, leather straps with various pulleys, pads from baseball mitts, and pillows to enable him to compress, rotate, or lift various parts of the cranium.

Each experiment took many weeks to conceive and design; the equipment was adapted specifically to suit each hypothesis. In this particular instance, he lay upon a V-shaped headrest using straps connected to his foot to increase the compression on the back of the cranial base. In this configuration he took himself to the very point of unconsciousness before releasing the pressure.

His first feelings as he came around were: *"A sensation of warmth"... " And also, a remarkable movement of fluid, up and down the spinal column, throughout the ventricles, and around the brain."*

Two important things were now clear to him. The first was that cerebrospinal fluid (CSF) movement was not circulatory, as assumed, but fluctuated.

The other was that there was a movement in the sacrum, that the sacrum was essential to, and aligned with, the normal movement of CSF in the cranium.

Here he concludes is the mechanical manifestation of primary respiration. To repeat that – 'primary respiration'.

This experiment and many others were repeated many times to check his findings. The initial model put forward is this: Will feels, at this time, like the movement is brought about by what he calls the *"reciprocal tension membrane"*. This means one area of the cranium moves so the others must follow, like two sticks with a taut rope between them.

Essentially, the cranium fluctuates between flexion and extension. The cranium becomes taller and thinner, and smaller and wider, with accompanied nutation and counternutation of the sacrum (essentially, the sacrum rocks forwards and backwards around a specific point).

He describes how a flexion pattern *"would simulate lifting the eaves of the roof of a barn and drawing them laterally. In the movement, the top of the central area of the roof would sag."*. This is the shorter and wider movement; extension is, of course, the opposite.

We must bear in mind that these movements are felt through the whole body.

Will begins to study as many heads as he can by looking closely at the people he encounters and at his patients.

Obviously, this might have made him come across as a little strange, but Will, it would seem, was not concerned with such trivial matters.

He sees that the cranium is anything but symmetrical in everyone he meets, causing most people to have different sized orbits, for example, affecting their eyesight.

Will concludes that certain birth strains, genetic anomalies, dentistry, and traumas can, if left unresolved, create issues with the movement of cranial bones, and therefore the movement of CSF in the cranium. This would lead to specific areas of the brain becoming compressed, affecting the development and function of the brain in these areas.

To confirm and research this, he brings about every kind of torsion that he knows of, in himself, multiple times – and documents the effects. Then either he or Adah would restore normal function again through the gentle techniques they are learning about.

Will starts to successfully treat patients with acute migraines, sinus disorders, epilepsy, hay fever, birth strains and even, at times, severe anxiety.

All were treated by tracing specific strains back to a previous event and correcting the strain to restore normal function to the cranium.

As I have said, it is not the purpose of this book to teach people to treat others, so this treatment description is necessarily vague. Cranial osteopathy has gone on to help thousands and thousands of patients internationally, from babies up to people aged well over 100 years old. However, as I say, it is far from being accepted in the medical world even now.

I personally would add that there are also, in my mind, two main groups of craniosacral osteopaths.

One group primarily works within a mechanical framework.

One group excepts a higher form of Intelligence to guide the treatment.

Both groups can produce good changes in patients. Still, for me, the mechanical model is limited in its scope to the parameters of thinking. It is still normal for a doctor to choose to give a baby drugs as a treatment for "reflux" rather than refer to a cranial osteopath and try and address the underlying causes naturally.

Will and Adah finally decided to speak publicly about their findings in September 1929. Much to their disappointment, nothing much happens. They are met with almost complete apathy.

Will is undeterred. It wouldn't be until 1942 before things started to move, as osteopaths began to understand cranial osteopathy's potential through the success of following the ideas within their own practices.

Within the osteopathic profession, there was then, and still are now, many practitioners that have never seriously looked at this way of working and often mistrust it.

This is taken out of the recent Oct/Nov issue of 'Osteopathy Today' printed by the IO, the Institute of Osteopathy. It is taken from an article on p50:

"Now what about those cranial types who claim to detect undetectable rhythms...".

We have a long way to go!

Will was someone who just knew Wholeness and naturally saw people as having a body, soul, and spirit. Still, he never got caught up in the ideas of organised religion or religious dogma. The journey that he went on felt outside of his control and felt predestined. He once commented to Adah after she asked why he must risk his health with direct experimentation: *"I am doing this because there is some reason I must. It has been so the entire way, and this is but one more step. I have been taken care of, and I know that protection will continue. Amazing things are opening up. I haven't been bought this far only to be let down. There is no need for fear or doubt."*

Adah also says of Will: *"...characteristic qualities of the man himself should be highlighted for your understanding of him. Because he was as he was, he did as he did. The fact that for so long a time he pursued a path of research, with no specific reason other than an underlying drive and an intuitive sense of direction he could not disobey, would appear to be a rare manifestation of inner orientation, faith, and self-discipline. Material acquisition was of minor importance as a motivating purpose throughout his life.*

Each day, and this was frequent, he turned to what he alluded to as "pause-rest" periods; periods of silence with no outward evidence of activity. This was done with utmost simplicity and naturalness. From these contemplative oases there came some of his most productive reasoning and results. It is why he said with entire sincerity, "This cranial thought is not mine." He liked the phrase "listening to silence" and used as an analogy the composer who makes as powerful use of silences as he does of sounds – of "communicative silences."

Two fresh tennets upon which he drew for nourishment of inner resources were "Be still and know" and "Closer is He than breathing."

When the period of teaching arrived, he referred to these on occasion with unaffected naturalness because they were an integral part of his philosophy and his daily living. Dr. Sutherland had no denominational affiliation but ...he was affiliated!"

Here again, we see echoes of Jiddu Krishnamurti and Andrew Taylor Still.

Will is a person who knows they are in an ocean of Wholeness, who has no fear of anything; not out of bravado, but because there is nothing to be fearful of. He naturally trusts and follows the path that Intelligence lays out for him. He is invigorated by it and is therefore passionate about his work, full of energy, and does not need or look for external approval. He knows what his role is and trusts in it.

This amazing man takes this natural living state with him wherever he goes and into whatever he does.

"Be still and know".

When he begins to treat using only the pressure of a "silk handkerchief", he becomes aware that although he may start a treatment in a particular place, the body will proceed to also restore balance in other parts of its own accord and in its own order.

It always goes towards Health and towards cause.

He intuitively learns from an aspect of silence or the ocean, which he refers to as "Dad".

His work, like Still's, becomes quiet and based not on the application of knowledge but on the direction laid out in the moment.

At the end of Will's life, his students and colleagues come to understand that Will has moved away from the mechanical model of primary respiration to working purely with the ocean or silence.

The quote I love of Will's is, *"When all the fulcrums are aligned, there will be peace and harmony"*.

As with Andrew Taylor Still, William Garner Sutherland's work is still not recognised as it should be.

This work, when you are not following a prescriptive mechanical approach, cannot be tested via double-blind trials, which is the industry standard. Double-blind trials can, by their very design, only test repeatable processes. Holistic practice can, at the moment, only be assessed by its clinical outcomes. This is because we allow the whole person in the context of their innate 'Health', which is supernatural, to come to a perfect neutral.

This is a perfect balance point that only relates to that person at that moment. The neutral is not an end in itself, but a place where a person can start to move forward again and renew.

What is necessary in that context, in that person, in that minute, will never be repeatable. It cannot be repeatable.

Up until now, clinical outcomes are not sufficient for much of the scientific community. Remember that science is a valuable tool to help us understand the World around us, therefore we need to constantly learn how we can adapt science to the World.

The common narrative now is, if the thing we are looking at cannot fit into our specific ways of measuring it (because it is complex and not repeatable) then it doesn't really exist and is called 'unscientific'!

There is no doubt that William Sutherland was scientific. However, like Still before him, he knew its limitations, and when treating and thinking, he used *"Be still and know"* and let silence be his guide.

Chapter Eleven

Dr Jealous and the Health

I hope the readers with an intimate knowledge of Osteopathy will forgive me for only speaking about three specific individuals.

I know there are many osteopaths that are and have been invaluable in progressing the profession. That is, as they say, 'a given,' and I mean no slight to those not mentioned.

For me personally, the most important influences in my journey have been silence, my patients, and Jim Jealous DO, who sadly passed away in February this year 2021.

William Sutherland had found and documented the effects of Primary Respiration on the human body. He showed how you can treat without the use of force (a giant jump forward) and expanded the understanding bought to us by Andrew Taylor Still that the cause of disease was 'withering fields'.

Sutherland showed that the balance you can achieve naturally without force was significantly more powerful and accurate than what can be achieved with it.

Will, like Still, also showed us that to be most effective, the practitioner needs to work from the landscape of silence or meditation (in Krishnamurti's parlance).

He proved there is a rate to primary respiration within the body that is palpable and that when the body is compensating, it will be happening around specific fulcrums (points in space). Simply put, he found a way of working with body, mind, and spirit as one. Will showed us how spirit and matter interrelate in a tangible and quantifiable way.

In the 1970s, a book was released by German embryologist Erich Blechschmidt. It had the catchy title of *"The Ontogenetic Basis of Human Anatomy: A Biodynamic Approach to Development from Conception to Birth."* I'm guessing you might have missed it.

Blechschmidt is obsessed with what is driving the development of the embryo. He understands we are forming within the context of the genetic fields but what is driving it? He refers in the book to *"biodynamic fields"* that are a *"mystery only known to the embryo"*, stating that these biodynamic fields are what is driving development.

Jim Jealous DO and his colleagues look at Blechschmidt's work, which continues today with people like Brian Freeman and Jaap van der Wal. They understand from Sutherlands and Stills work that the body can reposition itself towards normal if you work in a particular way with thoracic or primary respiration. Still, no one is sure what the Intelligence is behind the corrections.

The predominant model put forward in osteopathic courses is still a mechanical one. However, it is clear that William Sutherland had moved away from this. In the place of a mechanical model, words like energy are spoken about concerning this kind of event. For a start, everything could be viewed from the perspective of energy. It is essentially a non-specific statement. What kind of energy is being referred to – Electrical, kinetic, sound, light, entropy? Are these energies, of themselves, capable of Intelligence? Do they not follow very specific patterns of behaviour? Can they change shape and form? Are they of themselves intelligent? The word energy is very unsatisfactory when used in this way.

William Sutherland had spoken about something he called *"liquid light"* within the cerebral spinal fluid. Was there Intelligence inherent in the CSF? This was, at that time, a working hypothesis.

Jim Jealous DO and colleagues ask if these biodynamic fields are what is driving the embryo's development. Is it possible that they continue in our growth, development, and healing after birth?

Suppose they are what is driving our development. Why are we trying to dominate treatments by deciding what we want to happen? What if we were to hand complete control to the biodynamic fields, and how would you do that? What are the landscapes and the source of the fluids?

So, our journey continues.

Since the 1970s, Biodynamic Osteopathy has grown in its understanding. It is in a position to offer some answers to these questions.

The number of osteopaths working in this way internationally has grown steadily with the teaching of the Biodynamic phase courses that take a minimum of ten years to complete in full. The findings have been checked and re-checked thousands and thousands of times by thousands of people over decades.

I am going to discuss with you the parts that are relevant to our understanding of ourselves. This new understanding may help us answer the question, 'Can I change internally, radically, psychologically to learn how to renew our bodies and minds?'

We will start by looking at the biodynamic fields. The first thing you need to know about the biodynamic fields is that they are as much you as your body and mind.

Secondly, this whole area is going to be new to most of you and will therefore challenge everything you thought you knew about yourself.

Later in his life, Sutherland spoke about the idea that the fluids could lesion, and if they did, the physical body would *"lock up"*. He also said that the fluids had *"unerring potency"* that they are incapable of making a mistake, that they are perfect. This is what Still understood in that moment of epiphany *"I saw that the word 'God' signified perfection in all things and in all places"* that the fluids can diagnose and treat with perfect precision and force.

There are written examples that infer that this was how Still was able to diagnose so accurately. We have first to understand that we have, in essence, two fluid bodies, one that is perfect 'The Health' and one that is capable of compensation.

Without the ability to compensate, we would not last 5 minutes, but we would have no direction without the Health. If I was to cut my arm with a knife, the body would heal along well-known physiological lines, but how does the body know when to stop healing? When it marries with the health!

Note that in perfect balance, 'normal', we would have neither two fluid bodies nor a tissue body.

All would be one.

The fluids are not literally fluid like water and do not behave like water but are best considered as the ground substance of life, a protoplasm. They are conscious and incredibly Intelligent. Remember, embryologically, in conjunction with the genetic fields and silence, they develop the nervous system and every other part of you and exist, therefore, before the brain.

Sutherland describes the fluids as not being framed by human hands. They are the ground substance of every living thing brought to life by silence. If you can imagine, the fluids create the space, and the body grows into the space.

The health via the fluids creates a midline and a perfect matrix in the shape of your body. They create the segmentation of the body, along with everything else, and the stem cells form the tissue – Ectoderm cells at one pole, and Endoderm cells at the other, with Mesoderm cells filling in between the two.

Your nose is shaped as it is due to the fluids creating the space and the nose forming. This will be dictated by the Health, and the genetic fields will be a compensation to perfect form. Otherwise, all noses would be the same.

When the fluids have had to compensate for any reason, they will change shape and tone in order to affect the tissue body, physiology, and neurology. This is a difficult thing to fully imagine: that in the end, our tissue body can be moved and held in different positions and states by the fluids.

A common and understandable question from my patients is, *"Will this actually move the joints and muscles that are tight or restricted?"*

It can be hard to imagine that the fluid body can alternate its state between being very solid, if function demands it, to being absent of tension and more like a vapour, everything shifting as it moves towards the image created by the Health passing through the fluid body which will be relevant to that person in that moment.

This is how health works. The implicit order in Wholeness manifests in us at any given moment and guides us back to health. This re-balancing only takes place in a genuine state of neutral.

Rest allows us to access neutral and continue to grow and develop, to unfold as is intended, irrespective of what is happening to us or around us.

In the end, when you look at the soma (the tissue body) from the perspective of molecules and atoms, you see that we are 99.99…% space. As we said, if you were to increase the size of a single atom to the size of St Pauls Cathedral, the nucleus would be the size of a cricket ball and the atoms would be like flies buzzing around the outside. The rest is just space.

Here's an interesting question: what holds something together to form what we perceive to be a defined object, whether a human, a tree, or a rock? It is silence, the Health, and the fluids that are responsible for this, and they, as with everything else in the Universe, are constantly unfolding in relationship with the Intelligence implicit in the whole. Order.

Our task then is to be able to feel our own fluid body and the Health and learn to perceive the World through it. This will allow us to stop only processing the World from the landscape of thinking and shift us to a landscape of Wholeness without using force or will-power. This landscape is full of stillness, love, and silence. As we rest here, we are centred. We finally understand that we cannot centre ourselves. In this landscape, we can discern our true selves not as defined by our minds but by Divine Intelligence.

In this landscape, we are not confused. In this landscape, we can say, "We are wholeness"! This is the landscape of freedom put forward by Krishnamurti.

This is the landscape of meditation. When we are here, we are free, we are passionate, we are whole, we are free of fear, and we want to be of service.

Here there is no need for rules, laws, or dogma. They are completely redundant in this landscape. Anarchy, but in its purest sense.

Here we can all relate to each other and the World around us harmoniously. Here is the answer to the question 'What is normal?'

Normal is a supernatural state of neutral, where all the fulcrums are aligned, and you have peace and harmony. We can find this landscape when we learn to feel our fluid body and perceive the World through it.

The fluid body builds around a midline and permeates through you, and when healthy, continues through the skin to form a circle around you.

The fluids move only as a whole. The fluids need regularly to return to neutral in order to re-balance, because they can lesion in response to external and internal events. This is how trauma is held in the body and mind, sometimes for decades.

Without returning to neutral, the fluids will lose internal potency and become weakened. The fluids can remould, reposition, and re-arrange the body when at neutral. As we have said, the neutral will align you to silence, with the ocean, with what Krishnamurti describes as Intelligence, a Divine Intelligence, a consciousness separate from and on a completely different level from mind.

The fluids will express primary respiration and will have a rate. We can learn to feel this natural inspiration and expiration of primary respiration both in ourselves and in the ocean.

Lastly, when we are neutral and in the landscape of silence, you will experience no tension of any kind.

When I am treating, I will gently lay my hands on the body. Normally the shoulders. When I am completely silent, I can feel the shape and tone of the fluid body, the rate of primary respiration in the person, how much potency is present, and where it is located – what unresolved issues the body is most concerned about at that moment.

You can feel what is happening in the nervous system, respiration and many, many other things. Although, when the treatment begins, I am not focusing on or analysing any of it.

I sit in the silence with the Health in that moment.

This area of biodynamic osteopathy is challenging to learn and to properly understand. The training takes many years to be at peace with, often after your osteopathic degree. My only intention is to give you what you need to expand your understanding of yourself.

If you are interested in working in this way, you need to complete the studies or you will likely hurt those you are trying to help.

This is not a concern when we are just learning to view and be ourselves.

If we are fortunate enough to reach the landscape of meditation and have an understanding of Wholeness, know what real Love is, we can relate to each other outside the landscape of thinking, of words, and of images. We are where we need to be. We will start to know who we are and what we are here for, and we will have the drive, passion, and lack of fear necessary to achieve it.

We are always moving forward and developing. We are never perfect, or we would be stuck.

We will have changed radically, internally, psychologically!

Osteopathy has illuminated fundamental truths that we are all free to experience and explore for ourselves, in ourselves.

They are entirely consistent with Krishnamurti's ideas, but they also show how these truths are expressed through us, which makes finding the landscape of meditation and ourselves easier and means we don't need to be mechanical in our processes.

"We are not trying to be enlightened; we are only trying to be ourselves."

To be ourselves is to be a unique part of the whole and therefore not the same as anyone else. Any form of imitating, conforming, or blindly following dogma or rules will move us away from ourselves.

We must learn to trust the silence as it expresses itself through us and stand alone in the context of the Whole, with Love, with passion, in service. Order. Remember Rumi said: *"You are not a drop in the ocean you are a drop that contains an ocean."*

I would like to expand on the idea of the 'Health'.

As viewed from an osteopathic context, the Health is the physical manifestation in the moment of the divine intention of silence or the ocean. If we are trying to see it or understand it from the landscape of thinking, we won't be able to. There is Health in every moment, in everything. In the landscape of meditation it will be obvious. It is a person's essence. It is guiding the constant movement of order as it unfolds. There is no endpoint at which we reach the perfect, and that is it. It is in continual motion. To quote Jim Jealous DO: *"...imperfection is the leading edge of the perfect."*

Jim was my main companion in this journey through courses with him and all his recorded lectures and writings, all bought to life in my patients and myself through silence.

He was an amazing man, and I am very grateful to have known him. He took on the challenge of continuing the work of Andrew Taylor Still and William Garner Sutherland. True Osteopathic treatment is still rare in the World, as there are relatively few true osteopaths (there are many allopathic osteopaths). Its benefits are still, therefore, underutilised, and our understanding of its potential is still in its infancy. When it is fully realised, people will look back at these three osteopaths. They prove to us not only that we can renew (that means even after severe trauma) that we can change radically, psychologically, inwardly, but it also shows us how!

A couple of days before Jim passed away, he was talking to his close friend Gary Roba and he said *"Very little of life's events have any real meaning as seen from the other-side; in fact they hardly exist at all from that point of view, because the only thing that truly matters is Love. All there is on the other side of the veil, is Love."* If you want to know if you are with the Health, you are, if there is true Love in it. If it is an uphill battle, you are not.

The weekend after Jim died was the first sunny spring day for us here in my part of England, and I was out walking with my dog. I was at some point aware of feeling Jim. He was breathing out, he was happy, and there was a twinkle still in his eye.

Chapter Twelve

An ego-driven world, allopathic medicine, and psychology

I wanted to give you some examples of how my patients might present to me and how my view might differ from an allopathic one.

When I was studying for my original degree, I was told how a patient might present with a lot of pain on one side of the low back, pelvis and hip region, only to find that x-rays would reveal the opposite side to have significant arthritic change in the hip joint – not the side that was most painful.

They would look at me with a certain degree of surprise as they relayed this. Certainly, at the time, I was not able perfectly to articulate why this makes complete sense.

Think about how the fluid body is constantly moving and adapting to the unresolved matters within us. As that hip joint starts to deteriorate (let us say in this example on the left side), a process that would typically have begun many years before, possibly due to physical trauma or normal wear and tear, the fluid body will intelligently isolate the area to prevent that dysfunction from spreading wildly through the whole.

Then, among other things, the fluid body will move the centre of gravity to the person's opposite side.

Now, let's picture this. The right side of the body now has to work much harder from head to foot on that side. The tone and shape of the fluids will change to bring this structural shift and change in function into being.

Within these types of compensations, many things will be happening. Still, we will limit our focus for the purposes of this discussion to the areas that are causing the patient pain and restriction in this picture.

If we start at the pelvis – this is a common misdiagnosis point – the pelvis can move and adjust itself to allow our weight to go to either side, forwards and backwards, or any combination therein.

It is common for someone to be diagnosed with a structural leg length difference, when in fact it's just that the pelvis is being held by the fluid body in a specific compensation. This would mean that the legs are the same length, but the compensation in the pelvis makes it appear otherwise.

In the example we are discussing, where the fluid body is holding the centre of gravity to the right, the left side of the pelvis will likely be rotated backwards, with the left leg rotating out as if it is being held away from the body. The right side will be held in a very strong position mechanically to aid the increased weight-bearing.

If you lie someone down with this kind of compensation and gently roll the legs inwardly, you will find that the left side will move very easily and fluidly (If the hip permits). The right side will be very tight due to all the extra work the muscles are doing and, of course, the increased tone in the fluid body.

Here, patients might come across the reductionistic diagnoses of piriformis syndrome, tight iliotibial bands, or greater trochanteric bursitis (which become frequently compressed in these kinds of compensations).

It is essential to see that these diagnoses are not inaccurate, but they are only picking out a fraction of a much bigger picture.

Piriformis muscles don't just suddenly decide of their own accord to be tight all the time for no reason! They are tight because they are responding to the fluid body and a greater overall compensation.

Suppose we see a tight piriformis or trochanteric bursitis as problems in their own right, unrelated to anything else.

In that case, we never find the cause and we never really genuinely resolve what is happening in this person. It is not uncommon, in fact, for people to be operated on without looking for a cause. This, of course, often makes things considerably worse by adding new levels of tissue damage, and with it, more complex patterns of compensation.

In this situation, it is typical for people to have steroid injections into the trochanteric bursae, often making matters much worse. Even if the injection works, it is only allowing a compensation to remain unchanged and unchallenged.

It is easy to see that if the pelvis is rotated in this way. So that weight-bearing is predominantly on the right side, the lower back is now away from its normal position. The joints and ligaments, and muscles on the right side will be under increased compression in this example.

Here we come into direct contact with Still's *"withering fields"*. Suppose, for example, the person in question had a degree of arthritic change in the lower spine, which is true of everyone to a certain extent after a certain age. In that case, this might be enough to cause nerve irritation, affecting normal function in the right leg and pelvis, including the pelvic viscera.

The trouble is that allopathic medicine often does not see the big picture or overall pattern, let alone know how to help it. They too often see these problems as being separate from each other. They will then either tell you your muscles are weak, which they might or might not be, they might start injecting you with various cortico-steroids or place you on strong pharmaceuticals which are in no way curative and cost a lot of money.

So, the pelvis has shifted to the right in this example, which means that there is not only increased load on the right leg, ankle, and foot but on the outside of the leg, ankle, and foot.

This compensation will give rise to diagnoses of tight iliotibial bands or knee pain (the knee will be rotated relative to the tibia and compressed). Increased weight-bearing will also load the ankle and the foot due to the short-term leg length difference, all of which will, in the end, lead to some kind of pain and dysfunction; and in the long-term, more arthritic change.

To prevent me from becoming too detailed here, we haven't, in this example, looked at what would be happening in the upper body, neck, and head; but the compensation will be felt in every part of the body. In every cell.

This example also assumes that the person we are looking at has no other unresolved issues in the body at the same time, which is highly unlikely.

It is vital to understand that tension in the body is anything physical or emotional that has remained unresolved.

These physical tensions can be of mainly emotional origin; they do not have to have a physical cause. It would be normal to see many different unresolved patterns of compensation of multiple origin.

We can quickly see how a reductionistic allopathic approach is so narrow and unsatisfactory in many cases. In the end, if we are ill or in pain, it's the body's way of telling us something needs to change. It is a healthy process (With the exception of pathologies of genetic origin). If we constantly ignore the messages, greater problems will follow.

If, however, we were to work with the Health in the fluid body (That is to say, the perfect) to help find a neutral, the body would bring itself back towards balance again and would start to resolve the issues at their cause. This would bring the structure back towards normal function and position, removing the associated tone in the muscles and ligaments.

We would also have to rest, of course! once the left hip has really become too damaged due to osteoarthritic change years later. That is when surgery and evidence-based practice will become appropriate and vital. Though after the surgery, it will be working with the fluid body and the physical body that will restore normal function and Health.

The fluid body, as Sutherland said, has *"unerring potency"*. The Intelligence and precision we have as part of our normal function is mind-boggling in its capacity to restore physical and emotional balance. Sadly, we do not understand it or work with it. We are content with pumping ourselves full of various expensive and non-curative drugs instead.

If your car could fix itself, would you still take it to the garage?

The following example will look more at the effects of trauma in regard to the fluid body, the body, and the mind.

Due to the nature of my work, it is not unusual for a patient to present to me with significant physical pain that has, at its root, significant emotional or physical trauma that may have been present for many years or decades.

I will give you an example of a patient I have been treating recently as it is a fresh memory. This person came with significant low back pain and rigidity throughout the whole body; they could not sleep or function normally. As I started to help their fluid body re-balance and come to a neutral, it became apparent that the whole person had been overwhelmed entirely in every sense of the word. It really is in these cases that nothing is as it should be. The fluid body and, therefore, the body was completely solid in its tone to an extreme level. The autonomic nervous system was entirely stuck in fight or flight, and the physiology was a long, long way from homeostasis (balance).

The whole body moved as it released and eventually came to balance in a neutral.

In writing, it is impossible to convey the extent of what is happening in the whole person in these situations, nor the extent to which the Ocean has to work to achieve genuine perfect change in this one person.

As I am treating, I am entirely neutral and sitting with the Heath. It is no good me sitting there feeling emotional about the person's plight. This will not help them. Afterwards, though, after they have gone home, I reflect on what I have felt, and it is enough to make you cry. It is difficult to imagine how hard it must be on a day-to-day basis for anyone to live in this position. It does, though, like magic, find a neutral. It does start to change. Things do begin to resolve, start to renew.

Initially, after a week or so, the pain and rigidity began to settle in this person, and the patient was no longer in constant pain and could move much more freely. Often, after the first treatment, if it is not clear before, the memory of the original trauma or traumas begins to return. It is now possible that the effects of these traumas can start to be resolved.

I won't need to discuss the details with the patient, but they are often told to me for context and often just to tell someone neutral. This way of working is the opposite of psychology. Over time, the effects of these traumas on the person are slowly burnt away, not through talk, not through psychological concepts or forgiveness, but naturally, and quietly, through stillness.

You don't need to forgive someone for things to resolve, although this might well happen naturally. You just need the trauma to stop having an effect on you, so you can be free.

This will have an extraordinary effect in the end. The mind will begin to find quiet spaces between thoughts and emotions. The body will start to feel free, and mobile, and without tension. Then will come the time where the person is connected back to their 'Health'. They will be present, joyful, and finally aware of what they are really capable of and, more importantly, who they really are. They are suddenly aware of how amazing they are. How the viewpoint they had been carrying of themselves is in fact inaccurate and small when compared to the truth.

This won't be felt in an arrogant or cocky way, as they will also understand they are part of a whole, that their natural abilities are meant to operate in that context. They will start to live fully, freely, and no one will be able to take that away.

What is most upsetting about working in this way is that virtually everyone lives in this reduced state of being, which is caused by varying degrees of trauma and conditioning.

It is in all of our capacities and natural abilities to resolve this and live freely. I know that in the millions and millions of serious cases around the World only a small number, as it stands, will get a chance to discover this for themselves. They will therefore remain trapped and stuck until they die. All the potential and joy in those people is lost!

What is stopping this way of working from happening on a large scale is mechanical reductionistic people, their processes, and their inability to move beyond the confines of their own minds.

It is time for this to be challenged openly and honestly. To quote Charlie Chaplin in the great dictator: *"Don't give yourself to these unnatural men - machine men with machine minds and machine hearts! You are not machines!"*

Allopathic medicine and modern psychology, on the whole, fail to understand that we are not machines.

Generally, in the World of psychology, you have the professional, operating from their accumulated incomplete knowledge that is by nature full of bias, concepts, and assumptions.

Looking at a patient through this incomplete knowledge, they try and make the person better. Talking can help us gain some level of context and understanding about our histories, but as we have said, the word is not the thing. The models and ideas created through talking can, if not wildly inaccurate, really help the patients, and are an important aspect of the overall resolution. Still, talking in its self does not resolve the underlying trauma.

Suppose the models offered to the patient are wildly inaccurate, which they can be. In that case, they can be very damaging and add considerably to the patient's problems.

In the parlance of Krishnamurti, they are trying to restore order from within thinking – something we have shown to be impossible.

I want to talk about a couple of other examples.

I am not cherry-picking the people I talk about in these examples; they are people who have walked through my door in the last 2 weeks.

The example I would like to give now is a person I would describe as stuck. They absolutely do have an unresolved low back pain, which is part physical and part emotional in its origin.

From their perspective, they see themselves as being stuck in this space. They believe, therefore, that their body is not healthy enough to have this problem! They see no way that this might be fully resolved. Within themselves, they cannot come to a point of rest, and they are ill at ease.

We are increasingly understanding now that the brain operates as a filtering system. This translates to the idea that the more the brain is working, especially in an area of the brain known as the 'default mode network', the more it is filtering out the World internally and externally. In this situation, the mind loops round and round in often increasingly negative spirals, unable to move on. Recent studies suggest that the brain is in fact primarily a filtering system! EG, the harder the brain works, the less we can perceive.

Imagine a day in this person's life when rigidity of thought, found here, will also mean rigidity in the fluid body. It too will have become stuck, 'locked', and will be in a significant state of compensation.

The fluids are unable to come to neutral in this situation: the greater the unresolved traumas that sit behind the patient's issues, the greater the compensations. This will, in general, lead to rigidity through the whole body.

Neurologically, they are caught in fight or flight – with generally high neurological tone, the physiological functions will be affected in many different ways with changes to gut function, hormone levels and immunity, to mention a few.

Now, suppose this person is treated for low back pain in a reductionistic way. In that case, none of this background will even be seen, let alone addressed. They will be given multiple drugs that will mask the problem and endorse their idea that they are not healthy and can never be fully healthy or happy. This is further compounded by telling the patient they are also weak, more often than not in a structural sense. To be told you are weak or vulnerable when you are not well can be a considerable block to getting better.

When we suffer from pain, disease, anxiety, or depression, it is your body telling you something is not right. Something is not properly resolved that needs resolving before we can move forward again: emotional or physical trauma or, most likely, both.

If we do not heed this, the problems will continue, but we will also continue to add to them, and they will get bigger and bigger.

From here, the person will remain stuck in circular thought processes that are part of all these uncomfortable changes. They will start to make worse and worse decisions both about themselves and in relationships with others. They will be more likely to drink too much, overeat, take recreational drugs, or be in bad relationships.

These are desperate attempts to bring about peace and order. It is easy to see how things can spiral out of control from here, physically and emotionally.

CBT, and often a Freudian approach, are frequently prescribed in these situations, if anything is offered at all, alongside more drugs.

Suppose a person is stuck in circular thought processes, full of unresolved trauma and suffering physically. How is CBT going to change anything? We are not learning to live like this. We want to resolve it!

Other areas of psychology are far more promising. Carl Jung, for example, had a different approach. His model of an individual is a nice one. Essentially, he would say that we are born our true selves and that this true self meets the World around it and has to adapt to survive. This leads to the development of a false self built around the ego. The ego is essential here. It enables survival. The greater the hardship placed upon this child and adult, the more extensive the level of compensation, the more they will reside in the false self.

He would then place these two sides of self into a wholeness capable of restoring balance.

This is consistent with osteopathic findings that if we want things to change, we need to be guided by the Health in the situation (The perfect). This has nothing whatever to do with emotions or applied knowledge. We need to bring what is present in this person to a neutral, then from here, naturally through the Health. This circular pattern of misery can start to change naturally in the proper order and at the right pace.

Dr Gabor Mate, who is leading the discussion of trauma and its effects internationally, is helping considerably to get this message out. He is an amazing man and speaks beautifully on this subject and many others.

It is interesting to reflect that certain people become fulcrums for certain ideas and areas of thought – a literal point of reference. I think it's unlikely that they would have set out to achieve this; perhaps it is their role in the World.

Gabor Mate is a holocaust survivor as a young child. His grandparents died in Auschwitz. He was born in Hungary in 1944 during the NAZI occupation. Trauma was very present in his life, and that of his family, and those around them. He is now a retired physician living in Canada.

He has written many books on the idea that trauma is the origin of disease and mental illness not linked to genetic factors. He worked for over ten years in Toronto in an area infamous for very severe drug addiction. It became clear to Gabor the connection childhood trauma has on too many of our personal issues.

A study done in the UK in 2015 showed that 49% of children in care will end up in prison. In the UK at that time, 29% of the prison population had suffered childhood abuse, 46% came from homes where they had either experienced or witnessed violence.

Almost the entire prison population has experienced mental health issues, homelessness, suffered abuse or violence as a child, was addicted to drugs, or grown up in care. This shows that we do not look after our vulnerable members of society. We criminalise them instead.

Gabor maintains that only a tiny percentage of people who try drugs become addicts. This includes heroin. What unites addicts is underlying unresolved trauma. As a society, we are not recognising when things are going wrong for individuals and instead only see the criminality that often derives from it.

He shows, what is evident when I work, that most issues people present to me with, even if they seem mechanical, have an emotional core. Studies have shown disease is caused by either genetic anomalies, external bacteria or toxicity; then there is a large group titled 'idiopathic'. This means that, to allopathic medicine, it has no known cause.

Another study on this subject showed that the more racist attacks experienced by the black American women who took part in the study, the higher their likelihood of experiencing asthma.

Another similar fact is that children who grow up around stressed parents are also more likely to experience asthma. The more adverse childhood experiences a person has will directly increase their likelihood of having lung cancer, even after you have removed the effects of smoking from the figures.

A study in Canada in fact showed that if you were abused more than twice as a child, your risk of cancer went up by 50% – again, even after you have cancelled out the effects of smoking, drinking, drug-taking etc. This whole issue is not adequately understood in allopathic medicine. Trauma can also take place in many other less obvious ways. In the end, the effects of society and its belief systems on us is bound to lead to childhood trauma – not intentionally, but because we fundamentally have the wrong idea about what we are and what the World is.

Gabor is interested in how psychedelic drugs might help individuals see past their trauma, which is shaping them and their worldview.

Robin Carhart-Harris is carrying out the leading work in this area to ascertain whether this is true and how it might work. He has recently completed a study through Imperial College Oxford looking at the effects of psilocybin relative to escitalopram, an SSRI anti-depressant, in helping people with long term acute depression.

It was a small study whereby half of the participants continued taking escitalopram daily for 6 weeks with 2 doses of 1mg of psilocybin 3 weeks apart; the other half of the study had 2 doses of 25mgs of psilocybin and a placebo daily for 6 weeks. Due to previous connections of psychedelics bringing on psychosis, the people involved in the study were very carefully vetted before their involvement.

The BBC did a documentary on the research and featured a few of the participants as they went through the process. It's challenging to make the study blind as it is essentially apparent to most people in the study whether they had or had not had a psychedelic experience. However, it still allows them to look at the differences between the two treatment types to a certain extent.

What was clear from the BBC documentary was that for the people that it helped, the change in them occurred through the person having a spiritual awakening: not as put forward by Timothy Leary through being able to adapt to the World around us by rewriting our personal reality tunnels within a personal context of what we perceive to be right, wrong, or desirable.

Any genuine change that happens through the psychedelic experience occurs because it allows the person to have a clearer view of Intelligence and Wholeness, allowing them a more spiritual view of themselves and the World around them. This is an incredibly important distinction, as any change brought about through personal subjective ideas of good and bad will be severely limited.

I fully understand that this approach might be the right one in certain appropriate cases and we cannot learn about different treatment types if we don't look at things properly.

I started this book looking at Timothy Leary, who definitely studied this approach. Is history repeating itself? I want to know if the people involved in this work are looking beyond the mind? Can they understand that real change comes when the person involved can build a relationship with Wholeness and their true selves. Why are we always looking externally in order to change?

In the context of Biodynamic Osteopathy, it is possible for structural pain and dysfunction and physical and emotional trauma to be resolved without the use of external force or drugs.

When treatment takes place, it allows a pre-ordained process that will be done with perfect precision, force, and timing in the context of the person at that moment, all via a natural process.

I have just come in from treating a 4-week-old baby girl who was sleeping too much and not feeding, often for 8 hours at a time. She was unsettled in herself and often seemed uncomfortable. The birth had been relatively quick, the little girl had not been breathing at birth and had to be helped. This had been done quickly and successfully.

When we are first born and begin to breathe, this brings about a massive ignition and a cascade of change. At birth, we go from floating in lovely warm fluid in a nice safe space. Our mums do all our breathing, eating and drinking for us.

Then, all of a sudden, we are exposed to gravity and have to breathe for ourselves. In this little girl, the ignition had not happened fully due to the problems with the initial breaths. The treatment bought about this full ignition. Not because I planned it, but because that is what was needed.

How would this have happened with regular treatment? All babies should be treated with cranial osteopathy to iron out the effects of being in the womb and the birth process, to resolve things from the start.

Don't let babies have to grow around the compensations picked up before and during their birth.

What is happening to make all the changes I am referring to?

If we return to the story, I told you about how I started with this work. I was treating and had the extraordinary experience whereby my eyes began to shake. The room was lit with subtle light. What was happening at this moment was what we call a "stillpoint" and then a "deep neutral".

Stillness is a transmutational process that comes out of the silence/ocean when required and when we invite it. It can come in many different forms, possibly infinite, and the change it will induce will be specific to the person and the moment, never to be repeated.

Once the desired change has been achieved, it will dissipate back into silence. Stillness is a felt presence. It holds you; it transmutes. When you are in the landscapes of stillness, it changes you. It is very hard, impossible in fact, to convey in writing the amazing nature of stillness and what it is capable of. My challenge to you is to discover it for yourself, which will happen if you continue to rest, and practice perceiving the World through your fluid body.

Treatment via a biodynamic Osteopath will facilitate this process for you while you are not able to.

Having a relationship and understanding of stillness is vital to understanding the potential of Biodynamic and Craniosacral Osteopathic treatment.

In most cases, we do not need pharmaceuticals, surgery, physical manipulation, or psychedelics to heal and renew. We have all that we need naturally: "Our own medicine cabinet", as Andrew Taylor Still stated all those years ago.

The only thing stopping this from being fully present in our lives and in our cultures is that we are still obsessed with the fact that we have to drive all change through willpower and the application of knowledge.

And that anything spiritual is separate from science and as such has no relevance.

It is naivety that should no longer be left unchallenged, when millions are suffering unnecessarily from the effects of trauma and ill health – and we have the ability to ease this from a place of Wholeness. Which is a spiritual landscape.

At what point do we say that to refuse to advise treatment outside of a reductionistic, evidence-based practice viewpoint is negligent?

I am aware that no one can treat outside of their own experience, and I would not expect them to. Still, the continued obstruction and public denouncement of anything outside their experience and reductionistic science is the problem.

Coming back to allopathic medicine, it is dogged by only viewing us in terms of our symptoms, viewing us in a purely mechanistic way.

Here in the UK where I live, the NHS has for many years had the ideology that you are *"Treated by the system, not the person"*.

This couldn't be more mechanical in its approach. In most UK doctors' practices now, you are encouraged to only mention one issue at a time at each appointment, as if the idea that there might be a connection between symptoms was impossible!

Put yourself in the position of a doctor in this system. You have an average of 5 to 10 minutes for the entire appointment, which might not even be a face to face appointment.

You have been taught that it is better to have a mechanistic process when forming a diagnosis and treatment plan, especially if you are recently qualified.

Whether Doctors agree with this approach or not, they are not given the option to do otherwise.

So, imagine you are a doctor, and I come in with a particular complaint, let's say headaches. You have five minutes and not many options. You have no time to understand the context of the problem. You don't know me. You don't know what is unresolved in me. You have a fixed budget and are therefore reluctant unless necessary to refer for further examination.

Once you check, the headache is not a result of a brain injury, tumour, stroke, encephalitis, etc. The only options are to do nothing or prescribe. So, often they prescribe.

Who are the real winners in this system? Has the system met and understood the person in front of them to the point that they have got to the cause of the issue? What happens now that the problem has not been resolved but masked?

What if this was a serious presentation of severe anxiety, depression, or unresolved trauma? What if this person's life is falling apart? Send them for a bit of CBT?

People take drugs, recreational or otherwise, because they are lost, isolated, and in pain physically and emotionally. They are trying to remove themselves from the situation via disassociation. They are self-medicating.

Do we bother to find out what has happened to this person and offer them genuine understanding and help? No. As Gabor Mate's work shows, we tend to criminalise them instead. We are taking no responsibility as a society for what has happened to them.

The recent explosion in depression and anxiety in children is because they are lost within a bad culture, and all of us are responsible.

If we believe that the answer to these problems is pharmaceuticals, CBT, a bit of Freudian psychology and/or prison, we are sadly mistaken.

It has long been evident to me that the above mechanical system will lead to fewer and fewer face-to-face doctor's appointments. After all if they are only going to operate in a mechanical way, why not let an algorithm do it?

This needs, though, the acceptance on our part that our medical data be shared with various external businesses, mainly in IT. This has been a problem here in the UK until now while everyone is still in various states of lockdown concerning the present COVID 19 situation.

The UK government have announced, very quietly, that each person has only six weeks to fill out a hard-to-find form and return it to their doctor. Otherwise, their medical information and that of their children, if applicable, will be permanently and irreversibly given to NHS digital to do with as they please. This has, as I write, been reversed and extended, but the point remains – the powers that be want it done.

The ship is sailing away fast. Personal care is being taken away from our lives and replaced with huge contracts, paid for by you, to large pharmaceutical and IT firms.

They are cutting out the middleman.

You, the patient!

Chapter Thirteen

Wholeness

The World is a cruel, violent, and severely unfair place for most of its inhabitants

While the wealthy continue to become richer and more powerful, everyone else's fortunes diminish at the same time as the Earth itself.

The Earth's ability to support human life due to the actions of humans is declining rapidly. As I write this, the World's richest 1% own 43.4% of the World's wealth, growing every day. The country that tops the charts of millionaires is the epicentre of neoliberalism, America. There are, as I write, 7.9 billion people in the World, and the wealthiest 1% has more than twice the wealth of 6.9 billion of them.

Almost half the World is living on less than $5.50 a day. Billions of people live with no security, no future, and no hope. This picture is set to become far, far worse with rapidly approaching environmental change and the continuation of neoliberalism.

At the beginning of this book, I asked if we can change radically, psychologically and internally because, as Krishnamurti said in his talk in 1978, if not, there is no future for man, obviously.

In this book, we have looked in detail at what is consciousness, who we are, what is really meant by 'true self', and more importantly, Wholeness. We have looked at how we might start to explore this for ourselves through the body, mind and spirit that are always with us in a real and palpable way, free from any theories, religious dogma or conditioning.

Wholeness is a real landscape. Everything is one. As we speak, we live in a world that pretends this is not so. We are living in an illusion.

David Bohm said something like, *"the only thing everyone can agree on is that they do not believe in wholeness"*!

As long as we continue to buy into the illusion of separation created in the mind by the ego, there is no chance of change happening.

What can I tell you here about Wholeness? It cannot be felt from the perspective of the ego. Only as we start to process the World outside of our thinking can we start to feel Wholeness.

In this landscape, as we wait with no intention or plan, the body, mind and spirit are brought together again. They become one. We are a unique part of a whole and we are suddenly aware of it.

We are not trying to become something in time. We are ourselves now. We are aware in this landscape that all is one; but first, we must let go of what we know, of all our plans, of all our conditioning and trust. We learn that we are not weak but that we have far less power than we believe.

In the landscape of Wholeness, you are aware of the movement of Love. Not romantic love. Not your love for someone, or someone loving you, but real Love.

At this point, it would be worth asking how is this happening? What is the source? As the mind becomes transmuted and the observer leaves, all is one. All is whole.

We realise we are Wholeness.

We must not treat this experience as we would a fairground ride. It is not entertainment. It is something to take seriously. If we rest and wait, and trust, we will change radically, psychologically, internally!

Chapter Fourteen

Change

If we want to change radically, internally, psychologically (as put forward by Krishnamurti) the reality of Wholeness has to be with us always, however faintly, not as an idea but a living, breathing reality inside us – where we are at peace within its movement.

Love it for everything it does for us, to trust it implicitly.

In this space, we need no leaders, no authority, no dogma, no religion. We just need to feel our own unique movement within the whole as it unfolds.

When we look around us at the World, we quickly see that the dominant ideology is that 'thou must be successful!' – that the ego is God!

We learn at school that to pass exams is what learning is all about. You must be good at everything that we as a society, tell you you should be good at. You must be wealthy; you must be a winner.

This obviously breeds a worldview that infers that it is you vs everyone else. That you are on your own. It is a world full of judgement, discrimination, and prejudice. It's a world where opportunity directly affects your chances of succeeding in this society – where "life coaching" actually translates to working out how to become wealthier or more powerful relative to those around you.

A very brief Socratic analysis can disprove this in 5 seconds flat.

If being rich and powerful is the aim of life and defines a 'good' human being, then Donald Trump is what we are aiming at!

I recently watched a documentary about the England cricket team in the years after 2009. It was a moment of great success for the team resulting in them becoming the number one team in the World. The documentary showed how the single-mindedness and commitment it took to achieve this great success was, in the end, unsustainable. It ultimately led to a number of mental breakdowns within the team that were largely ignored and, in the end, punished.

Increasingly we see this pattern repeated in professional sport, with more and more athletes finding themselves in difficulties mentally.

We are starting to see that this blind ambition in our World, in ourselves, is not healthy and was not there when we were born.

There is no such thing as original sin. You are born compassionate, loving, and full of joy. It's not our nature that's bad. It's our cultures.

We are conditioned. Education should first and foremost be about learning who we are – what are the gifts naturally given to us? – not wedging people through arbitrary hoops, not defining what skills are good and what are bad, not strangling the life and passion out of someone before they have even had a chance to know themselves.

The loss of potential and the disorder this brings are crimes against humanity and the World they inhabit.

In the end, all of the above is done to continue the wealth collection and standing of the supremely wealthy.

It is a modern form of slavery.

Education needs to be a safe space where children can explore themselves and the World around them without judgement. This is what a lot of the teachers also want.

We cannot have a rigid syllabus when we have no idea who or what each person will become; or what the World will look like.

This rigidity is only present to support the insane economic ideologies that are the leading force in the World as we find it now.

We end up with a domineering system that tells children what is and isn't right, what is and isn't important. It is impossible to imagine what the World would look like if we were all free to bring our natural selves and skills to bear on the World, free from the arbitrary lines we have drawn as a society.

It is time we found out what we have been missing.

This World can be seen as a world of opposites that come to define each other, yin and yang. They are different sides of the same coin.

Within this sea of opposites there are things we interpret as bad and things we interpret as good. Death, for example. You cannot have life without death.

We are not looking to create a world which only consists of what we personally interpret as good. What would happen if nobody ever died?

Would you really describe this world without death as good? Mark Zuckerberg and Jeff Bezos might!

In this book, we have looked at the spiritual aspects of ourselves and the universe. We have looked at the World and ourselves from the perspective of science. It is the wrong question to ask, "Which of these two is more important?"

Neither way of perceiving the World is more valuable than the other. They are both one when we live in a world that only values a reductionistic worldview, as we do. It means that we are only ever looking at a fraction of the whole.

When you present to your doctor, teacher, employer, or psychologist, most of the time they see only you and themselves in a reductionistic way. They are looking at a fraction of the whole, and only from their perspective, refusing to accept there is any more to know. At which point in our development as a society do we deem this attitude to be negligent and challenge it openly?

We have seen how traumatic experiences in our lives can have far-reaching adverse effects on our health, and therefore what happens in the course of our lives.

Biodynamic Osteopathy, amongst other things, has shown that these traumas can be, and are meant to be, resolved naturally. We have no need for applied knowledge, force, or analysis for this healing to occur. We can change radically, psychologically, internally, but only if we step out of our tiny little universes that we have put together in the landscape of thinking, and let them Die.

We need no longer accept a world that discourages our own humanity, a world that is specifically built to condition your mind so you can no longer see or even remember your true self – a world set up to rob you of ever knowing yourself, or ever knowing Wholeness, of ever knowing Love.

We can no longer accept a world narrative that focuses solely on one side of the coin. For me, a purely spiritual viewpoint that I will label a "new age" viewpoint is just as damaging as a purely reductionistic one. We need both, and we require that they both be given equal credence as they are correctly seen as part of the same whole.

We can live within Wholeness, not as an ideology but as a felt truth, as a living, breathing landscape. This means that we realise that what Krishnamurti describes as "Intelligence" – which can also be described as "God", or "the Devine", or "the great Creator", or "Tao", or "Buddha Mind" – is implicit in everything, in the universe, including you and that within this, order is implicit.

If you look at the environmental issues that we have, they exist because we are getting in the way of a natural implicate order, oblivious to the harm we are doing.

We get in the way because we believe that we have to, that the World would fall apart without us, or we act as it benefits us personally in the moment – even though we know that the Earth is over 4.5 billion years old and that homo-sapiens have only been on the Earth for 200,000 years and things were working just fine before.

We delude ourselves that we can generate perfect order, as we would like to have it or believe it should be, through our fragmented incomplete knowledge. We just cannot let it go.

As we have seen with our previous discussions, order cannot be found within thinking. We only create greater levels of disorder.

It is common when I speak to people about the idea that we can be much greater, more complete versions of ourselves, that they say: "Isn't that a bit utopian?"

We have to decide whether allowing yourself and others to live in a world that does not allow us to be ourselves, to know ourselves, that is hell-bent on destroying itself, is utopian? Or whether these doubts and, in fact, words, are just another aspect of your continued conditioning?

Go and find out for yourselves. See for yourself. At the start of the book, I quoted:

"We are not trying to be enlightened; we are only trying to be ourselves."

If we all do this. The rest will look after itself. As described in this book, we can first rid ourselves of our past traumas and find Wholeness in ourselves through natural processes. We, at this point, won't need leaders. We won't need Nation. We will not only be free, but we will understand that we can, by being ourselves, be of great service to others and the Earth at large and that this is a duty.

The people in charge now wrongly believe themselves to be intelligent, based on the knowledge they have acquired and the opportunities they have been given.

They do not understand necessarily how limited this intelligence is. Often, they are successful in the context of our culture, reaching positions of power and accumulating wealth. This further reinforces their egos' ideas of their inherent superiority relative to others, and therefore the assertion that it is only right they should be in charge – that they should decide what our laws are and how society works and is ordered.

Individuals will have specific knowledge that will be of use to us as a society, but because they are operating outside of the context of Wholeness, they are only concerned with their own wealth, power, and fame. They do not care that they contribute to the destruction of the World around them as long they are alright. That they survive.

The massive increase in technical and scientific knowledge combined with an ego-driven competitive World is driving us faster and faster towards the destruction of man. It continues to lead to extinction on a daily basis. The people in charge in this World stand for the continuation of this destructive pattern. Most of these people only rise to positions of power by conforming to these ideologies, by proving they will not rock the boat.

The question of what political party to vote for is the wrong one. The right question is: Why do we need political parties at all?

In revolutions, we see historically that when one power base is removed, it is the group or groups who have cohesion and organisation at that moment who eventually take over.

Most of the time, they introduce a system that is worse than what was previously in place. Revolutions classically bring horrendous violence, destruction, and fear. None of this will happen if we unite together in sufficient numbers, in Wholeness.

In this landscape, we will just come together and quietly take control back by simply not recognising the old structures, laws, and boundaries.

By learning to live and interpret the World and ourselves through the Health in any given situation, through our hearts, we are whole. We are changed.

It has long been a vital question how the worlds of spirit and matter interact? Do they interact? You can now find out for yourselves. No need to take anyone's word for it. I have described how through Biodynamic Osteopathic thinking we can build a relationship with the Health in the whole of ourselves and, therefore, Wholeness, that we can begin to feel the quiet voice of Intelligence and, therefore, what our direction should be. I have free mediations to help you with this process online.

We are all born with a divine essence. No one is more divine than anyone else. Original sin is not true. We are all born good. We are all part of a whole movement present throughout the whole universe and beyond. We are saying, to be clear, that the fluid body is as much a part of you as your body and your mind. That spirit, mind and body are one. That within those fluids lives divine perfection, the Health.

The time has come to find this reality in yourself, for all our sakes. To learn to know yourself.

I will leave you with the speech given by Charlie Chaplin in the Great Dictator – his response to Hitler's Nazi Germany and suppression of all kinds:

"I'm sorry but I don't want to be an empero

That's not my business

I don't want to rule or conquer anyone

I would like to help everyone if possible

Jew, Gentile, Black man, White

We all want to help one another, human beings are like that

We want to live by each other's happiness, not by each others misery

We don't want to hate and despise one another

And this World has room for everyone, and the good Earth is rich and can provide for everyone

The way of life can be free and beautiful, but we have lost the way

Greed has poisoned mens' souls, has barricaded the World with hate, has goose-stepped us into misery and bloodshed

We have developed speed, but we have shut ourselves in

The machinery that gives us abundance has left us in want

knowledge has made us cynical

Our cleverness, hard and unkind

We think too much, and feel too little

More than machinery, we need humanity

More than cleverness, we need kindness and gentleness

Without these qualities life will be violent, and all will be lost

The aeroplane and the radio have brought us closer together

The very nature of these inventions cries out for the goodness in men – cries out for universal brotherhood – for the unity of us all

Even now my voice is reaching millions throughout the World – millions of despairing men, women, and little children – victims of a system that makes men torture and imprison innocent people

To those who can hear me, I say – do not despair

The misery that is upon us is but the passing of greed – the bitterness of men who fear the way of human progress

The hate of men will pass, and dictators die, and the power they took from the people will return to the people

For so long as men die, liberty will never perish

Soldiers!

Don't give yourself to brutes – men who despise you – enslave you – who regiment your lives – tell you what to do – what to think and what to feel!

Who drill you – diet you – treat you like cattle, use you as cannon fodder

Don't give yourself to these unnatural men – machine men with machine minds and machine hearts!

You are not machines!

You are not cattle!

You are men!

You have the love of humanity in your hearts!

You don't hate!

Only the unloved hate – the unloved and the unnatural!

Soldiers!

Don't fight for slavery!

Fight for liberty!

In the 17th Chapter of St Luke is written "the kingdom of God in within man" – not one man, nor a group of men, but in all of man!

In you!

You, the people have the power – the power to create machines

The power to create happiness!

You, the people, have the power to make this life free and beautiful, to make this life a wonderful adventure

Then in the name of democracy – let us use that power – let us all unite

Let us fight for a new world – a decent world that will give man a chance to work – that will give youth a future and old age a security

By the promise of these things brutes have risen to power

But they lie!

They do not fulfil that promise

They never will

Dictators free themselves but they enslave the people!

Now let us fight to fulfil that promise!

Let us fight to free the World – to do away with national barriers – to do away with greed, with hate and intolerance

Let us fight for a world of reason, a world
where science and progress will lead to
all men's happiness

In the name of democracy, let us all
unite"

Epilogue

I said at the beginning of this book, I wrote it as a promise to the Ocean, which I have felt as an instinctual obligation. I hope that the book starts a conversation within yourself. I hope it creates change. For further information on meditations designed to help you feel the Edges" course, see my website: www.centeringaroundtheedges.com

There are guided mediations specifically connected to this book and my meditation courses available for free on my YouTube Channel: The Family Osteopath.

If you would like to contact me directly my email address is: Oliver@Familyosteopath.co.uk, or you can contact me via my Facebook page: Centering Around the Edges. Thank you. Oliver.

End Notes

Chapter One

A full list of the Books used to research this book is in the Bibliography.

Recording – YouTube – J.Krishnamurti – Official Cahnnel –

J.Krishnamurti – Madras 1978 – Public Talk 6 – Can the brain renew itself?

John Higgs writes in the end notes of I have America surrounded that he had taken most of the information around Leary's escape from prison from Leary's confessions of a hope friend, Flashback,and Jail notes. Leary had changed a lot of the details over the years to protect those involved.

I have taken the information regarding Timothy Leary from Leary's Flashbacks, and High Priest, and John Higgs's I Have America Surrounded and further reading on various websites. The quote sources are as follows:

"I never knew my grandparents on the Ferris side. They died in the influenza outbreak of 1918, leaving the diminished acreage and two farmhouses to my Aunt Dudu, a timid, fanatically religious gnome who futilely tried to direct family affairs with Irish-village piety, sitting on a couch all day clicking her false teeth, mumbling prayers, and reading Catholic tracts. As befitted her venerable status as ruler of the household, Aunt Dudu slept in the master bedroom, called "Grandfather's Room" in honor of the doughty little farmer-tyrant who built it." Flashbacks p25

"hot and sassy" Flashbacks p25

"Never do anything like anyone else, boy." Flashbacks p24

Interpersonal diagnosis, this description was researched mainly through Flashbacks p17, and John Higg's I Have America Surrounded p19,20,21, John used Robert Anton Wilsons definition of 'normal'.

Leary's research determining, No matter what kind of psychotherapy they used, a third of patients would get better, a third would stay the same, and a third would deteriorate further. Control groups, where no care was given, showed precisely the same results! What they were doing was not working. Flashbacks p16

"My Darling, I cannot live without your love. I have loved life but have lived through you. The children will grow up wondering about their Mother. I love them so much, and please tell them that. Please be good to them. They are so dear." I Have America Surrounded p22

"Tim's head was twice the size, completely swollen up, incredible! He couldn't see; his eyes were completely shut!" I Have America Surrounded p23

"I died. I let go. I surrendered. I slowly let every tie to my old life slip away. My career, my ambitions, my home. My identity. The guilts. The wants. With a sudden snap, all the ropes of my social life were gone." Leary, High Priest p9

"urging that we emphasize inner potential and personal growth through self-reliance, so patients avoid dependence on authoritarian doctors and dogmas."Flashbacks p17

"After half an hour, the effects of the drug started, and the world just came alive. Tim looked at Bruce, who was diligently writing down his observations and was struck by the realisation that Bruce had no idea at all what he was observing. He found this realisation incredibly funny, and the earnestness and detachment of the scientific community suddenly appeared to him as ludicrous ignorance. How could they even begin to understand something that they were so separated from?"

Higgs, I Have America Surrounded, p30. Note Leary gives a full account of his first trip in High Priest p11-34

Chapter Two

My Research regarding this chapter derives primarily from jkrishnamurti.org, and Lives in the shadow with J. Krishnamurti, by Radha Rajagopal Sloss, Krishnamurti, the years of awakening, by Mary Lutyens, From Atheism to Theosophy, by Annie Besant, and Wikipedia. Note Radha is the daughter of Rajagopal Krishnamurtis right hand man and Rosalind. She grew up in Ojai with Krishnamurti, and her mother and father.

The accounts Radha gives of Theosophy and of Krishnamurtis early life were largely told to her by her Aunt Erma – Rosalind's sister, her mother, and from direct discussions with Jiddu Krishnamurti. As with all spoken accounts we cannot be totally sure about the accuracy of events. As we have learned this will derive from Radha's reality tunnel, her own interpretation.

It should be noted that there is much confusion around these events and even Krishnamurti's date of birth is not agreed upon. Items mentioned regarding his early psychic experiences were recorded by Krishnamurti in memoirs

Quotation sources for this chapter are as follows:

"to a certain extent Psychic". p20 Lives in the shadow, R.R.Sloss

"seen her light her cigar, without matches or other observable assistance, while standing at the rail in the midst of a furious storm. Every other living creature had been driven below deck." p7 Lives in the shadow, R.R.Sloss.

"scrawny, dirty, cough racked, lice-ridden, crooked toothed with rickety legs" and "dim-witted" were both observations by a Theosophy scholar, Ernest Wood. p22 Lives in the shadow R.R.Sloss

"Do you see him?" p65 Lives in the shadow, R.R.Sloss

"in good spirits" and "told her many things" p88, Lives in the shadow, R.R.Sloss

"One of the greatest thinkers of the age" Tenzin Gyatso, 14th Dalai Lama, as quoted on the jacket of 'Inward Revolution, by J.Krishnamurti.

Chapter Three

In researching this chapter, I used the books referred to in the above notes about Chapter One, and Chapter Two. Information around Aleister Crowley was researched via The book of the law, by Aleister Crowley, Stranger than we can imagine, John Higgs, and blog.prepscholar.com.

Quotation sources are as follows:

"They're waiting for you!" Wikipedia.org, The Book of the Law, Summons.

"of deep timbre, musical and expressive, its tones, solemn, voluptuous, tender, fierce…".

The voice was said to have no "native or foreign accent". Wikipedia.org, The Book of the Law, Writing.

Dear Robert

How are you doing? I'm doing fine over here, but it's not what I expected. Too crowded.

Love,

Tim

I Have America Surrounded, John Higgs. John references Ram Dass speaking to Peter Gorman, 5th May 1996, p23 High Times: Timothy Leary Special Tribute Issue.

Chapter Four

I have read many books and articles in order to research this chapter, but the primary references were Profit Over People, by Noam Chomsky, The Shock Doctrine, by Naomi Klein, and A brief History of Neoliberalism, by David Harvey. A lot of my personal views are apparent in this chapter. Naomi Klein's 'The shock doctrine' is a must read for anyone interested in the form of modern economics and how it affects our world. I would highly recommend reading it.

I wondered whether to include this chapter in the book but in the end, it provides the ultimate context for why the modern world is as it is. Quotation sources are as follows:

"Washington consensus" As defined by Noam Chomsky in Profit over People. p19

The Washington consensus would overthrow Guatemala's first democratic government in 1954 for "stability" security for "the upper classes and large foreign enterprises," whose welfare must be preserved. p21 Profit over people, Noam Chomsky.

"Britain would not tolerate independent development in that region." p30 Noam Chomsky, profit over people.

Chapter Five

This chapter looks in detail at some of Krishnamurti's main observations. I haven't taken them specifically from any particular book or talk and is my interpretation of what he is saying. The primary books that I have read are The awakening of intelligence, by J.Krishnamurti. The first and last freedom, Jiddu Krishnmurti. Freedom from the known, Jiddu Krishnamurti. Wholeness and the implicate order, by David Bohm. Talks I like on YouTube are the conversations between Krishnamurti and David Bohm, and the 6 public talks Krishnamurti did in Madras in 1978. I would encourage you to find these yourself.

The rest of the information is just things I have learnt over the years and have pieced together here to make a specific point.

The 'Man is born in Tao' is credited to Chuang Tzu.

Information on Richard Davidsons research can be found on his website, www.richardjdavidson.com. A great documentary on this study is called A joyful Mind.

Chapter Six

Multiple Model Agnosticism is put forwards by Robert Anton Wilson which I first came upon in John Higgs book KLF: Chaos Magic Music Money. It offers us a way past the juxtaposition of knowing that all our models of thought are incomplete but still needing to rely on them at times.

Some of the information around time I knew but the quantum area I read about in Carlo Rovelli's book, The order if time.

Note the final quotation, "All statements are true in some sense. False in some sense. Meaningless in some sense. True and false in some sense. True and meaningless in some sense. False and meaningless in some sense. And true and false and meaningless in some sense." is also accredited to Gregory Hill, better known as Malaclypse the Younger.

Chapter Seven

Quote: "You have a plan. That's great, but it isn't going to work. We are more powerless, not weaker than we believe." This is a quote I wrote down during a lecture with Jim Jealous D.O but I am sure there is a similar quote in one of his recorded lecture series.

Quote: "you are not a drop in the ocean, you are a drop that contains an ocean." Rumi's full name is Jalal al-din Muhammed Rumi. He was a 13th century poet, scholar, and Sufi mystic from Iran.

Research around the Knepp estate and into 'Rewilding' came mainly from www.knepp.co.uk and Isabella Tree's book, Wilding: The return of Nature to a British Farm. Which is a truly inspirational book of great value to us going forward. I would highly recommend it to you.

Chapter Eight

Quote: "Anyone who knows this place is blessed." This is a Krishnamurti quote from the end of his 6th public talk in Madras 1978.

Chapter Nine

I have for years now had all of Andrew Taylor Stills books and to have listened to numerous lectures referring to both him as a man and also his work. The best book I have ever read about him though is John Lewis's, From The Dry Bone To The Living Man which you can purchase directly from him at www.atstill.com . I have taken inspiration and information definitely from this book and also from Still's writings; and talks and conversations I have had with other osteopaths.

Quote sources for this chapter are as follows:

'The explorer of truth must first declare his independence' A.T.Still p4

'He must establish his observatory on hills of his own; he must establish it above the imaginary high planes of rulers, kings, professors of schools of all kinds and denominations. He must be the Czar of his own mental empire.' A.T.Still p4

"They believed in self-control and complete honesty. Each person was his or her own judge, responsible not only for their own behaviour but for the behaviour of all. Elders were very respected. Children were taught that the Great Creator loves all equally and therefore to injure, wrong, or hate another was to injure oneself. To do good to another person and make them happy was to make yourself happy. They had no concept of ownership, of rich and poor. If you had more than you needed you gave it to those that needed it." quote regarding Stills time on a Shawnee reservation. A.T.Still p27

"The dead Indians never objected to being object-lessons for the development of science. Their relatives knew nothing about it; and as 'where ignorance is bliss it is folly to be wise,' and as the knowledge which I gained by this research has aided me to relieve countless thousands of suffering human beings, and snatch many from the grave, I shall not allow my equanimity of mind to be disturbed by the thoughts that I once sought knowledge from Indian bones."

"It was when I stood gazing upon three members of my family, all dead from disease, spinal meningitis, that I propounded to myself the serious questions: 'In sickness has God left man in a world of guessing? Guess what is the matter? What to give, and guess the result? And when dead, guess where he goes?' I decided then that God was not a guessing God but a God of truth. And all his works, spiritual and material, are harmonious. His law of animal life is absolute. So wise a God had certainly placed the remedy within the material house in which the spirit of life dwells." From Stills Autobiography p87-88

A "withering field". A term used repeatedly in Stills writings to describe an area of the body that was not operating from a position of physiological health.

For Still, when the body was ordered and therefore 'normal', it would be healthy. It had its own "medicine cabinet" terms used repeatedly in Stills writings

"Like a burst of sunshine the whole truth dawned on my mind, that I was gradually approaching a science by study, research, and observation, that would be of great benefit to the world". Foundations of Osteopathic Medicine p4

"All God's work is perfect" a quote Still remembered from preachers that turned into an important question for him.

"I was shot in the dome of reason by an arrow charged with the principles of philosophy. Since that day I have sacredly remembered and kept its anniversary... sometimes withdrawing from the presence of man to meditate upon the event of that day wherein I saw that the word 'God' signified perfection in all things and in all places." A profound insight that came to Still while in conversation with his brother Jim on Monday, 22nd June 1874. Essentially the birth of osteopathy for Still. Autobiography p258

"Science cannot deal with fundamental questions". and"Science is only a tool or a key, and it can unlock only certain material problems. It cannot appraise itself. It is not a judge but a witness. Problems of mind, of character, moral, aesthetic, literary, artistic are not its sphere. It counts and weighs and measures and analyses, it traces relations, but it cannot appraise its own results." A.T.Still p83

"you will find all that heaven and earth contain, fully represented, mind, matter and motion, blended by the wisdom of Deity." History of Osteopathy p463

"With the iron hand of will I barred the gate of memory, shut out the past with all its old ideas. My soul took on [a] receptive attitude, my ear was tuned to nature's rhythmic harmony... My spirit was o'erwhelmed with the unmeasurable magnitude of the divine plan on which the universe is constructed." Stills Autobiography p312

"Once in the operating rooms (treatment rooms) you are in a place where printed books are known no more forever. Your own native ability, with nature's book, are all that command respect in this field of labor. Here you lay aside the long words, and use your mind in deep and silent earnestness; drink deep from the eternal fountain of reason, penetrate the forests of that law whose beauties are life and death. To know all of a bone in its entirety would close both ends of an eternity.

Solemnity takes possession of the mind, a smile of love runs over the face, the ebbs and tides of the great ocean of reason, whose depths have never been fathomed, swell to your surging brain. You eat and drink; and as you stand in silent amazement, suns appear where you never saw a star, brilliant with the rays of God's wisdom, as displayed in man, and the laws of life, eternal in days, and as true as the mind of God Himself." Stills Autobiography p179

Ernest Tucker, "Could the spirits reveal the nature of God?" Still replied: "God is a term by all living beings spoken mentally or vocally, signifying that I am going to lift myself above the individual and personal limitations and thoughts, and rise to the broadest freedom of thought."

A.T.Still p310

"To your heart ever be true" A.T.Still p324

"It is true to the design of nature when we act our true selves." A.T.Still p303

Chapter Ten

As with Still I have had William Sutherlands books for many years now. This chapter is researched from Sutherlands books, the brilliant With Thinking Fingers: The story of William Garner Sutherland, D.O., D.Sc. (Hon.), written by Sutherland's wife Adah Strand Sutherland. Information about his early life comes from the book Journeyman by Jane Eliza Stark.

Quote sources are as follows:

"the thought came, like a bolt from the blue" William Sutherland explaining how the idea of cranial bone mobility came to him while looking at a disarticulated skull at the ASO.

“It must be something first, with something else second...we must get back to the spark that ignites the motor...get back to the central station, and reason. Take the creation of man; the Maker breathed the Breath of Life, not the breath of air, into the nasals of a form of clay and man became a living soul...the breath of life uses the breath of air as one of the material elements in a mechanism to walk about on Earth. The human brain is a motor...it will not be found in a laboratory....” notes of Will’s while thinking about his next steps regarding primary respiration. Thinking Fingers p35

“All the physiological centres including that of respiration, are located in the floor of the fourth ventricle.” more notes of Will’s regarding the same question. Thinking Fingers p36

“A sensation of warmth”...” And also, a remarkable movement of fluid, up and down the spinal column, throughout the ventricles, and around the brain.” Thinking Fingers p40

“I am doing this because there is some reason I must. It has been so the entire way, and this is but one more step. I have been taken care of, and I know that protection will continue. Amazing things are opening up. I haven’t been bought this far only to be let down. There is no need for fear or doubt.” Thinking Fingers p54

“...characteristic qualities of the man himself should be highlighted for your understanding of him. Because he was as he was, he did as he did. The fact that for so long a time he pursued a path of research, with no specific reason other than an underlying drive and an intuitive sense of direction he could not disobey, would appear to be a rare manifestation of inner orientation, faith, and self-discipline. Material acquisition was of minor importance as a motivating purpose throughout his life.

Each day, and this was frequent, he turned to what he alluded to as "pause-rest" periods; periods of silence with no outward evidence of activity. This was done with utmost simplicity and naturalness. From these contemplative oases there came some of his most productive reasoning and results. It is why he said with entire sincerity, "This cranial thought is not mine." He liked the phrase "listening to silence" and used as an analogy the composer who makes as powerful use of silences as he does of sounds – of "communicative silences."

Two fresh tennets upon which he drew for nourishment of inner resources were "Be still and know" and "Closer is He than breathing."

When the period of teaching arrived, he referred to these on occasion with unaffected naturalness because they were an integral part of his philosophy and his daily living. Dr. Sutherland had no denominational affiliation but …he was affiliated!" Adah Sutherland on Will.

"Be still and know". This was a famous saying of Will's. The full quotation is "Be still, and know that I am God" taken from the bible Psalm46:10

"When all the fulcrums are aligned, there will be peace and harmony" William Sutherlands famous quote to describe health.

Chapter Eleven

I was incredibly fortunate to have been able to study with Jim Jealous in studying some of his Biodynamic Phase courses in Oregon, America. This Chapter sets out to explain Jim's addition to osteopathic thinking. I have taken information from Sutherlands books here as well as from Jim's lectures that had with him, his recorded lecture series you buy from www.jamesjealous.com .

Chapter Twelve

Gabor Mate study carried out in the U.K and Canada and much more is covered in his book, The Wisdon of Trauma.

Chapter Thirteen

Information on the balance of wealth is taken from www.inequality.org

David Bohm quote is from his book, Wholeness and the Implicate Order.

Chapter Fourteen

Charlie Chaplin quote from The Great Dictator speech.

Bibliography

Becker, Rollin: The Stillness of Life.

Becker, Rollin: Life in Motion.

Besant, Annie: From Atheism to Theosophy.

Blechschmidt, Erich: The Ontogenetic Basis of Human Anatomy: A Biodynamic Approach to Development from Conception to Birth.

Bohm, David: Wholeness and the Implicate Order.

Booth, Emmons: History of Osteopathy, and 20th Century Medical.

Crowley, Aleister: The Book of the Law.

Chomsky, Noam: Profit Over People: Neoliberalism and Global Order.

Harvey, David: A Brief History of Neoliberalism.

Higgs, John: I Have America Surrounded: The life of Timothy Leary.

Higgs, John: Stranger Than We Can Imagine: Making Sense of the 20th Century.

Higgs, John: The KLF: Chaos, Magic and the Band Who Burned a Million Pounds.

Jealous, James: An Osteopathic Odyssey.

Kahneman, Daniel: Thinking, Fast and Slow.

Klein, Naomi: The Shock Doctrine: The Rise of Disaster Capitalism.

Krishnamurti, Jiddu: Awakening of Intelligence.

Krishnamurti, Jiddu: The First the Last Freedom.

Krishnamurti, Jiddu: Freedom from the Known.

Labatut, Benjamin: When We Cease to Understand the World.

Leary, Timothy: Flashbacks.

Leary, Timothy: High Priest.

Leary, Timothy: Turn On, Tune In, Drop Out.

Lever, Robert: Mind, Matter, Motion.

Lewis, John: A.T.Still: From the Dry Bone to the Living Man.

Lutyens, Mary: J.Krishnamurti. The Years of Awakening.

Mate, Gabor: When the Body Says No: The Cost of Hidden Stress.

Mate, Gabor: In the Realm of Hungry Ghosts: Close encounters with Addiction.

Mate, Gabor: Scattered Minds: The Origins and Healing of Attention Deficit Disorder.

Merton, Thomas: The Way of Chuang Tzu, 2nd Edition.

Merton, Thomas: Zen and the Birds of Appetite.

Murray, Nicholas: Aldous Huxley: An English Intellectual.

Nerburn, Kent: Neither Wolf Nor Dog: On Forgotten Roads with an Indian Elder.

Rovelli, Carlo: The Order of Time.

Seffinger, Michael. Dr.: Foundations of Osteopathic Medicine.

Sloss, Radha Rajagopal: Lives in the Shadow with J.Krishnamurti.

Stark, Jane Eliza: Journeyman: William Garner Sutherland, The Formative Years.

Still, Andrew Taylor: Philosophy of Osteopathy.

Still, Andrew Taylor: Autobiography of Andrew Taylor Still.

Still, Andrew Taylor: The Philosophy and mechanical principles of osteopathy.

Still, Andrew Taylor: Osteopathy research and practice.

Sutherland, Adah: With Thinking Fingers: The Story of William Garner Sutherland.

Sutherland, William: Teachings in the Science of Osteopathy.

Sutherland, William: Contributions of Thought.

Suzuki: Zen Mind, Beginners Mind.

Tagore, Rabindranath: The Realisation of Life.

Tree, Isabella: Wilding: The Return of Nature to a British Farm.

Tzu, Chuang: The Book of Chuang Tzu.

Tzu, Lao: Tao Te Ching.

Van Der Kolk, Bessel: The Body Keeps the Score: Mind, Brain and Body in the Transforamtion of Trauma.

Young, Ed: I Contain Multitudes: The Microbes Within Us and a Grander View of Life.

DVD's and YouTube Lectures:

Krishnamurti, Jiddu: J.Krishnamurti – Madras 1978 – Public Talks 1 to 6.

Krishnamurti, Jiddu: J.Krishnamurti – Rajghat 1981 – Public Talk 1.

Krishnamurti, Jiddu: J.Krishnamurti – Rishi Valley 1977 – Public Talk 2.

David Bohm with Krishnamurti – Ojai 1981, seminar 3.

Van Der Wal, Jaap: Embryo in Motion: Understanding Ourselves as Embryo.

CD's

Jealous, James D.O: Entire Lecture Series.

Printed in Great Britain
by Amazon

79809944R00109